CCTV 9
Chinese Program

D1359549

TRAVEL IN CHINESE

旅游汉语 ①

《旅游汉语》节目组 编

外语教学与研究出版社
FOREIGN LANGUAGE TEACHING AND RESEARCH PRESS
北京　BEIJING

图书在版编目(CIP)数据

旅游汉语. 第一册／中国中央电视台英语频道《旅游汉语》节目组编 . —— 北京：外语教学与研究出版社，2008.4
ISBN 978 - 7 - 5600 - 7496 - 2

Ⅰ. 旅… Ⅱ. 中… Ⅲ. 旅游—汉语—对外汉语教学—教材 Ⅳ. H195.4

中国版本图书馆 CIP 数据核字 (2008) 第 057571 号

出　版　人：于春迟
责任编辑：陈　轩
装帧设计：孙莉明
出版发行：外语教学与研究出版社
社　　址：北京市西三环北路 19 号 (100089)
网　　址：http://www.fltrp.com
印　　刷：北京华联印刷有限公司
开　　本：787×1092　1/16
印　　张：13.5
版　　次：2008 年 10 月第 1 版　2008 年 10 月第 1 次印刷
书　　号：ISBN 978 - 7 - 5600 - 7496 - 2
定　　价：75.00 元
＊　　＊　　＊
如有印刷、装订质量问题出版社负责调换
制售盗版必究 举报查实奖励
版权保护办公室举报电话：(010)88817519
物料号：174960001

《旅游汉语》出版人员名单

Consultant: Zhang Changming
顾问：张长明

Program Designers: Sheng Yilai Wang Xi
总策划：盛亦来 王晰

Chief Editor: Lai Yunhe
主编：来云鹤

Text Writers: Xin Ping Mark Rowswell (Canada)
撰稿：辛平 大山（加）

Translators: Cheng Lei (Australia) Zhu Xiaomeng
翻译：成蕾（澳）朱晓萌

出版说明

近年来，来华旅游、观光的外国朋友越来越多，为满足他们学习汉语、了解中国文化的需要，中国中央电视台英语频道基于多年汉语教学节目的编导经验，特别策划制作了一栏精品汉语教学节目——《旅游汉语》。中央电视台组织经验丰富的对外汉语教学专家进行教学内容的设计与编写，并特邀在中国家喻户晓的大山担任主讲。本节目在中央电视台首播后，收视率一直名列前茅，反响热烈，很多远在海外的观众希望早日出版该节目光盘以及配套教材。

应广大学习者的要求，中央电视台首先在黄金时间安排重播该节目，并与外语教学与研究出版社联合策划，推出了《旅游汉语》节目的系列配套教材和DVD光盘。

本系列教材以一个家庭在中国的生活为主线，强调语言与文化相结合，内容充实、实用性强，在华日常生活中的衣食住行、风俗习惯、旅游常识、景区介绍都包含其中，主持人大山风趣幽默的语言也给节目增添了许多亮点。

配套教材共分五册，每册附DVD光盘两张。每课正文分为以下六个主要部分：课文及英语译文、生词、重点词语注释、文化背景、语言点、句型与替换练习。

教材内容由浅入深，由易而难，五册书难度逐级递升，适用于所有以英语为中介语学习汉语的初级读者。学习者可以根据自己的实际汉语水平和需要选择适当的分册开始学习，配合教材并反复学习DVD光盘的内容，以期达到短期内提高汉语口语水平的目的。

外语教学与研究出版社

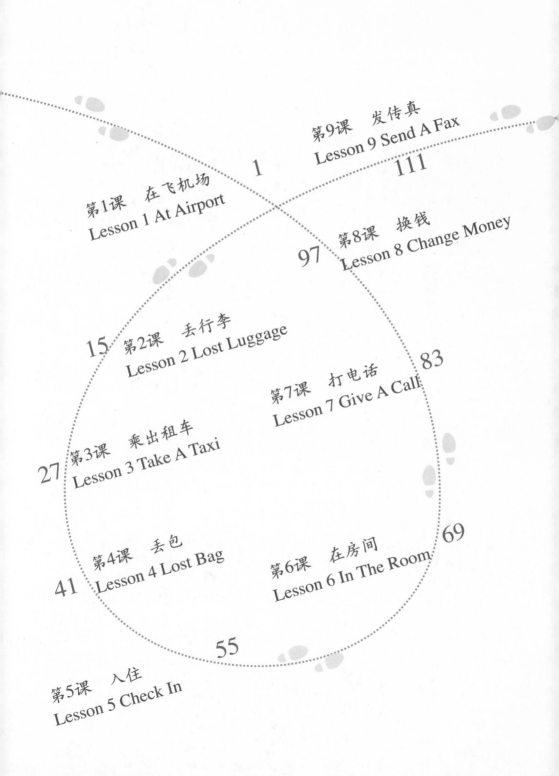

Contents

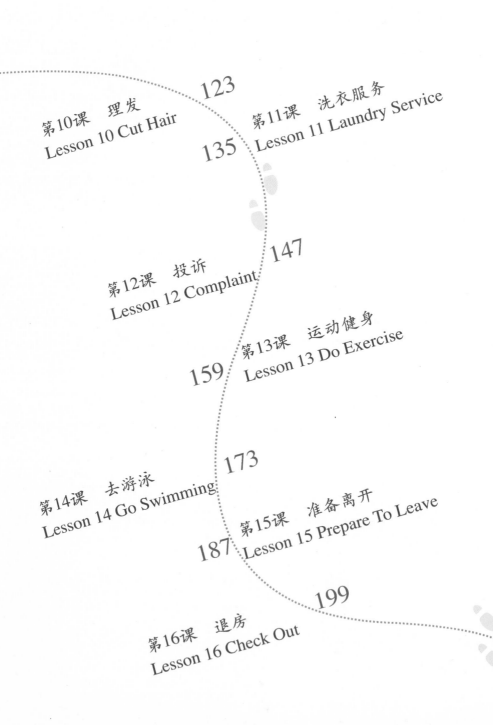

第1课

在飞机场
At Airport

课文 （Text）

Kōngzhōng xiǎojiě: Xiānsheng, dǎrǎo yīxià, zhè shì rùjìngkǎ, qǐng ná hǎo.
空中 小姐： 先生， 打扰 一下，这是 入境卡，请 拿好。

Huáng Rénháo: Hǎo, xièxie. Lái, yī rén yī zhāng.
黄 人豪： 好，谢谢。来， 一 人 一 张。

Xuěméi: Zhèlǐ xiě míngzi, zhè lǐ tián shénme ne?
雪梅： 这里 写名字， 这里 填 什么 呢？

Huáng Rénháo: Nǐ gōngzuò de dìfang, xiě gōngzuò dānwèi de míngzi jiù
黄 人豪： 你 工作 的 地方，写 工作 单位 的 名字就

kěyǐ le.
可以 了。

Xuěméi: Zěnme xiě a?
雪梅： 怎么 写 啊？

Huáng Rénháo: "Xīnwén Bàoshè", wǒ gěi nǐ xiě ba.
黄 人豪： "新闻 报社"，我 给 你 写 吧。

Xuěméi: Xièxie. Zhùzhǐ xiě nǎr?
雪梅： 谢谢。 住址 写 哪儿？

Huáng Rénháo: Xiě fàndiàn ba, fángzi hái méiyǒu zū hǎo, zhǐ néng xiān
黄 人豪： 写 饭店 吧，房子 还 没有 租 好，只 能 先

出入境的时候，应
该将填写好的出入
境登记卡、护照、
签证一起交边防检
查站检查。

zhù fàndiàn le.

住 饭店 了。

Xuěméi: Fàndiàn de míngzi shì "Míngyuè Fàndiàn" ba?

雪梅： 饭店 的 名字 是 "明月 饭店" 吧?

Huáng Rénháo: Duì. Xiǎojié, wǒ gěi nǐ tián ba.

黄 人豪： 对。小杰，我 给 你 填 吧。

Xiǎojié: Xièxie!

小杰： 谢谢!

Xuěméi: Zhè cì gōngsī pài nǐ lái Zhōngguó zhēn shì gè hǎo jīhuì.

雪梅： 这 次 公司 派 你 来 中国 真 是 个 好 机会。

Wǒmen kěyǐ zài Zhōngguó shēnghuó yī duàn shíjiān le.

我们 可以 在 中国 生活 一 段 时间 了。

Huáng Rénháo: Shì a, nǐ yě kěyǐ dào Zhōngguó gè chù qù kànkan.

黄 人豪： 是 啊，你 也 可以 到 中国 各 处 去 看看。

Kànkan zhēnshí de Zhōngguó.

看看 真实 的 中国。

Xiǎojié: Nǐ zuì hǎo duō xiě yīxiē wénzhāng, ràng wàiguórén

小杰： 你 最好 多 写 一些 文章， 让 外国人

hǎohāo liǎojiě Zhōngguó.

好好 了解 中国。

Xuěméi: Fēijī yào jiàngluò le, zuòhǎo ba.

雪梅： 飞机 要 降落 了，坐好 吧。

Huáng Rénháo: Zhōngyú huí dào jiā le.

黄 人豪 ： 终于 回到 家 了。

Biānjiǎn rényuán: Nín hǎo.

边检 人员 ：您 好。

Huáng Rénháo: Nín hǎo.

黄 人豪 ：您 好。

Biānjiǎn rényuán: Qǐng nín chūshì hùzhào hé jīpiào.

边检 人员 ： 请 您 出示 护照 和 机票。

Huáng Rénháo: Zhè shì wǒmen sān gè rén de.

黄 人豪 ： 这 是 我们 三 个 人 的。

Biānjiǎn rényuán: Nǐmen shì yī jiā rén ma?

边检 人员 ： 你们 是 一 家 人 吗？

Huáng Rénháo: Duì!

黄 人豪 ：对！

Biānjiǎn rényuán: Nín lái Zhōngguó de mùdì shì shénme?

边检 人员 ：您 来 中国 的 目的 是 什么？

Huáng Rénháo: Wǒ shì gōngsī zǒngbù pài lái de.

黄 人豪 ：我 是 公司 总部 派 来 的。

Biānjiǎn rényuán: Nǐmen dǎsuan zhù zài jiǔdiàn?
边检 人员：你们 打算 住在 酒店？

Huáng Rénháo: Gōngsī zhèngzài bāng wǒmen zhǎo fángzi, wǒmen
黄 人豪：公司 正在 帮 我们 找 房子，我们

zànshí zhù zài jiǔdiàn.
暂时 住在 酒店。

Biānjiǎn rényuán: Nímen dǎsuan zài Zhōngguó gōngzuò duō cháng shíjiān?
边检 人员：你们 打算 在 中国 工作 多 长 时间？

Huáng Rénháo: Gōngsī pài wǒ lái gōngzuò liǎng nián. Tā hé bàoshè yě
黄 人豪：公司 派我来 工作 两 年。她和 报社 也

qiān le liǎng nián de hétong.
签了 两 年 的 合同。

Biānjiǎn rényuán: Hǎo! Zhù nǐmen zài Zhōngguó guò de yúkuài!
边检 人员：好! 祝 你们 在 中国 过 得 愉快!

Xuěméi: Ài, xíngli zài nǎr ne?
雪梅：唉，行李 在 哪儿 呢？

Huáng Rénháo: Yīnggāi wǎng qián zǒu ba.
黄 人豪： 应该 往 前 走 吧。

Xuěméi: Hǎo.
雪梅：好。

We'll be home soon.

Stewardess: Excuse me, sir. These are the entry cards for you.

Huang Renhao: Thank you. Here, one each.

Xuemei: This is for the name, what do I fill in here?

Huang Renhao: Your workplace, just write the employer's name.

Xuemei: How do I write it?

Huang Renhao: Newspaper Office. I'll write it for you.

Xuemei: Thanks. What address should I write?

Huang Renhao: Write the name of the hotel, because we haven't rented a place yet, so we'll stay at the hotel first.

Xuemei: The hotel is called Mingyue Hotel, right?

Huang Renhao: Yes. Xiaojie, let me write it for you.

Xiaojie: Thank you!

Xuemei: Your appointment to China is really a great opportunity. We could live in China for a while.

Huang Renhao: You can also tour all around China and have a close look at a real China.

Xiaojie: You should write lots of articles, so people in other countries can understand China better.

Xuemei: The plane is landing. Sit well, honey.

Huang Renhao: We'll be home soon.

Customs Officer: Hello.

Huang Renhao: Hello.

Customs Officer: Please show me your passports and plane tickets.

Huang Renhao: This is for the three of us.

Customs Officer: Are you all one family?

Huang Renhao: That's right!

Customs Officer: What's your main purpose for visiting China?

Huang Renhao: I've been assigned here by the company headquarters.

Customs Officer: You plan to stay at a hotel?

Huang Renhao: The company is looking for a place for us, we'll be at a hotel temporarily.

Customs Officer: How long do you plan to work in China?

Huang Renhao: The company has appointed me here for two years. She has also signed a two-year contract with the newspaper office.

Customs Officer: That's good!Have a pleasant stay in China!

Xuemei: Where do we get our luggage?

Huang Renhao: It should be further ahead.

Xuemei: OK.

旅游汉语

生词（New Words）

1. 空中小姐	kōngzhōng xiǎojiě	名	air stewardess
2. 先生	xiānsheng	名	Mister (Mr.)
3. 打扰	dǎrǎo	动	disturb
4. 入境	rùjìng	动	enter a country
5. 填	tián	动	write, fill in
6. 新闻	xīnwén	名	news
7. 报社	bàoshè	名	press, newspaper office
8. 给	gěi	介	for somebody
9. 住址	zhùzhǐ	名	address
10. 租	zū	动	rent, hire
11. 派	pài	动	dispatch
12. 可以	kěyǐ	动	can
13. 真实	zhēnshí	形	true, real
14. 最	zuì	副	most, least, best
15. 好好	hǎohāo	副	in perfectly good condition

16. 了解	liǎojiě	动	understand, comprehend
17. 广播	guǎngbō	名	broadcasting,radio
18. 乘客	chéngkè	名	passenger
19. 着陆	zhuólù	动	land
20. 系	jì	动	tie, fasten
21. 降落	jiàngluò	动	land, descend
22. 出示	chūshì	动	show, sight
23. 护照	hùzhào	名	passport
24. 打算	dǎsuan	动	plan, intend
25. 暂时	zànshí	名	in a short period
26. 艺术家	yìshùjiā	名	artist
27. 愉快	yúkuài	形	happy, joyful
28. 行李	xíngli	名	luggage, baggage
29. 应该	yīnggāi	动	should, ought to

旅游汉语

注释（Notes）

1. 好好

"好"，作形容词时读第三声，重叠之后第二个"好"读第一声，表示认真或仔细地做一件事情。Do something carefully. 例如：好好听，好好看。

2. 我给你写吧。

You may know that 给 means "to give", but here it's used differently. Here, it means "do something for you" or "do something on your behalf " and is followed by the verb 写, "to write". So, 我给你写 means "I'll write it for you".

3. 我们可以在中国生活一段时间了。

可以 is a very common verb that indicates you can or are able to do something. Here it is used with the verb 生活, "to live". Now we can live in China for a length of time. No more short trips!

4. 应该

应该 is used to indicate that something should be possible. Xuemei wants to know where they can take their luggage, but Huang Renhao doesn't know the exact place, so he says "应该往前走吧", it should be ahead.

文化背景（Sign Posts）

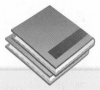

Beijing or Peking

You might get a little confused about the difference between Beijing and Peking. Is it Beijing duck or Peking duck, Beijing opera or Peking opera? Unfortunately, people use both terms and each side seems to think they are the most correct.

The Chinese name of the capital city didn't change, just the romanized spelling. In my view, Peking is just a wrong spelling that became popularized. The city's name is pronounced "北京" and should be spelt in English with a "B". However, the name Peking was used for many years and it stuck. Some people insist on using "Peking" because that's what they think foreigners are used to. Others use Beijing for the city name, but keep Peking for well-known names like Peking duck or even Peking University. Regardless, you can use either Peking or Beijing, but at least in my view, Beijing is preferable.

旅游汉语

语言点（Bookmarks）

1. 哪儿 where

你们住在哪儿?

Where do you live?

你从哪儿来?

Where do you come from?

哪儿卖火车票?

Where do they sell train tickets?

2. 给 for somebody

妈妈给儿子收拾房间。

The mother tidied the room for her son.

他给我介绍了中国的交通情况。

He told me all about transportation in China.

3. 应该 should do something

如果他坐两点的火车，现在应该到了。

If he took the two o'clock train, he should have arrived by now.

他是在中国长大的，应该看得懂中文。

He grew up in China, he should be able to understand Chinese.

已经是三月了，应该暖和了。

It's already March, it should be warm by now.

句型与替换练习
（Substitution & Extention）

1. 可以can, maybe, possibly

我可以用这个电话吗？

Can I use this telephone?

替换例句：

> 我们现在可以走了吗？
> ——可以。
> 我可以给你打电话吗？
> ——不可以。

2. 是……的 a way of emphasizing something

他是去年九月来的。

He came last year in September.

他是来旅游的。

He came for tourism.

他们是坐船走的。

They went by boat.

她是在家吃的早饭。

She had breakfast at home.

替换例句：

> 她是从法国来的。
> 他们是骑自行车去的。

第 2 课

丢行李
Lost Luggage

旅游汉语

课文 (Text)

Huáng Rénháo: Shǔshu, dào le jǐ gè xíngli le?
黄 人豪 ：数数，到了几个 行李 了?

Xuěméi: Hái shǎo yī gè, nà gè hóng de dà xínglixiāng.
雪梅：还 少 一个，那个 红 的 大 行李箱。

Huáng Rénháo: Kěnéng hái méiyǒu chūlái, tóngshí yǒu hǎo jǐ gè
黄 人豪 ： 可能 还 没有 出来，同时 有 好 几个

hángbān de xíngli, zài děng yīhuìr ba.
航班 的行李，再 等 一会儿 吧。

Xiǎojié: Wǒ qù tuī gè xínglichē guòlái.
小杰：我去 推 个 行李车 过来。

Huáng Rénháo: Hǎo.
黄 人豪 ： 好。

Xiǎojié: Kàn, wǒmen nà gè fēijī de xíngli dōu chūlái le,
小杰：看，我们 那 个 飞机 的 行李 都 出来 了，

yǐjīng shì xià gè hángbān de le.
已经 是 下个航班 的 了。

Xuěméi: Gǎnkuài qù wènwen ba, zěnme huí shì?
雪梅：赶快 去 问问 吧，怎么 回 事?

口语化的表达，问
原因的时候使用，
也可以说"怎么一
回事?"

Huáng Rénháo:
黄 人豪： Wǒ qù nàbiān de guìtái wènwen.
我 去 那边 的 柜台 问问。

Huáng Rénháo:
黄 人豪： Wǒmen shì gāng cóng
我们 是 刚 从

Měiguó lái de, wǒmen de xíngli shǎo le yī jiàn.
美国 来 的，我们 的 行李 少了 一件。

Gōngzuò rényuán:
工作 人员： Qǐng gěi wǒ kànkan nín de jīpiào hé xíngli piào. Sān gè
请 给 我 看看 您 的 机票 和 行李 票。三 个

rén de xíngli, yīgòng sì jiàn.
人 的 行李，一共 四 件。

Huáng Rénháo:
黄 人豪： Duì, xiànzài zhǐ yǒu sān jiàn.
对，现在 只 有 三 件。

Gōngzuò rényuán:
工作 人员： Kěnéng chūxiàn le yīxiē tèshū qíngkuàng, nín xiān tián
可能 出现 了 一些 特殊 情况， 您 先 填

yī zhāng biǎo.
一 张 表。

Huáng Rénháo:
黄 人豪： Shénme yuányīn ne?
什么 原因 呢？

Gōngzuò rényuán:
工作 人员： Xiànzài hái bù qīngchu, děng yīhuìr wǒ huì zài gěi nín chá
现在 还 不 清楚， 等 一会儿 我 会 再 给 您 查

yīcì. Nín shuō yīxià nà gè xínglixiāng shì shénmeyàng de.
一次。您 说 一下 那 个 行李箱 是 什么样 的。

乘飞机的时候，如果托运的行李找不到了，可以马上和机场的行李管理人员联系。如果是在北京首都国际机场，您可以直接和国际行李查询处(Lost & Found Office)联系。工作人员会帮助您和航空公司联系，找回您的行李。

Xuěméi: Hóngsè de, zhème dà de.

雪梅： 红色 的，这么 大 的。

Xiǎojié: Yǒu suǒ, hái yǒu yī gēn hèsè de dàizi.

小杰： 有 锁，还 有 一 根 褐色 的 带子。

Huáng Rénháo: Nà gè xiāngzi duì wǒmen hěn zhòngyào.

黄 人豪： 那 个 箱子 对 我们 很 重要。

Gōngzuò rényuán: Xiānsheng, duìyú chūxiàn de wèntí, fēicháng bàoqiàn.

工作 人员： 先生，对于 出现 的 问题，非常 抱歉。

Huáng Rénháo: Xīwàng jìnkuài gěi wǒmen yī gè dáfù.

黄 人豪： 希望 尽快 给 我们 一 个 答复。

Gōngzuò rényuán: Nín fàngxīn, wǒmen yīdìng huì jìnkuài chǔlǐ de.

工作 人员： 您 放心，我们 一定 会 尽快 处理 的。

Xiānsheng, qǐng liú xià nín de liánxì diànhuà.

先生， 请 留 下 您 的 联系 电话。

Huáng Rénháo: Diànhuà? Liú biǎojiě jiā de diànhuà ba.

黄 人豪： 电话？留 表姐 家 的 电话 吧。

Gōngzuò rényuán: Yī yǒu jiéguǒ wǒmen jiù tōngzhī nín.

工作 人员： 一 有 结果 我们 就 通知 您。

Huáng Rénháo: Hǎo, nà wǒmen jiù xiān zǒu le!

黄 人豪： 好，那 我们 就 先 走 了！

Gōngzuò rényuán: Zàijiàn!

工作 人员： 再见！

Huang Renhao: Have a count, how many do we have now?

Xuemei: It's still one short, the big red suitcase.

Huang Renhao: Maybe it hasn't come yet. There's quite a few flights arriving at the same time. Wait a bit longer.

Xiaojie: I'll go get a trolley.

Huang Renhao: OK!

Xiaojie: Look, all the luggage for our plane is out, this luggage is for the next flight.

Xuemei: Quick, you'd better go ask what's happened.

Huang Renhao: I'll go ask at that counter.

Huang Renhao: We've just arrived from the United States. We're missing a piece of luggage.

Staff: Please show me your plane tickets and luggage stickers. Three people's luggage, four pieces in total.

Huang Renhao: Yes, so far we've only got three pieces.

Staff: There might be special circumstances. Please fill out a form first.

Huang Renhao: What's the reason?

Staff: It's not clear right now. I'll check again for you in a while. Can you describe the suitcase please.

Xuemei: It's red, about this size.

Xiaojie: It has a lock and a brown strap.

Huang Renhao: That suitcase is very important to us.

Staff: We are very sorry about this problem, sir.

Huang Renhao: We hope you can give us an answer as soon as possible.

Staff: Rest assured, we'll handle it as soon as we can. Please leave a contact phone number, sir.

Huang Renhao: Phone number? We'll leave cousin's home phone number.

Staff: We'll inform you as soon as there is a result.

Huang Renhao: OK, then we're going!

Staff: Goodbye!

生词 (New Words)

1. 数	shǔ	动	count
2. 可能	kěnéng	副	possible, maybe
3. 再	zài	副	once more, again
4. 推	tuī	动	push
5. 赶快	gǎnkuài	副	quickly
6. 只	zhǐ	副	only, just
7. 出现	chūxiàn	动	appear
8. 特殊	tèshū	形	special, particular
9. 清楚	qīngchu	形	clear, distinct
10. 查	chá	动	check, examine
11. 重要	zhòngyào	形	important, significant
12. 对于	duìyú	介	with regard to, concerning
13. 希望	xīwàng	动	hope, wish
14. 尽快	jìnkuài	副	as quickly as possible
15. 留	liú	动	leave

16. 联系	liánxì	名	contact
17. 结果	jiéguǒ	名	result
18. 通知	tōngzhī	动	notify
19. 一……	yī...		as soon as
就……	jiù...		

注释（Notes）

1. 可能还没有出来。
Maybe it just hasn't come out yet. 可能，it's possible.

2. 再等一会儿吧。
Wait a little longer. 再 means again or more. Here it indicates a little longer.

3. 赶快去问问吧。
Quickly, go and ask. Find out what happened. You could say 快去问问吧, but 赶快 is more emphatic. We've got to solve this problem right away.

4. 请给我看看你的机票和行李票。
Please show me your airline ticket and baggage ticket.

5. 可能出现了一些特殊情况。
Maybe there is some special reason.

6. 等一会儿我再给您查一次。
Wait a moment, then I will take a look for you. Remember, 再 means again or more. 我再给您查一次。I'll look again for you.

7. 一有结果我们就通知您。
We will contact you as soon as we have news. 一有结果，as soon as there is some result. 我们就通知您，we will contact you right away.

语言点（Bookmarks）

1. 可能 possible, maybe

   这么晚了他可能不会来了。
   It's so late, maybe he won't come after all.

   今天下午可能会下雪。
   Maybe it will snow this afternoon.

2. 再 indicates an action or state repeating or continuing

   请您再说一遍。
   Could you say that again?

   我们再等一会儿吧。
   Let's wait a little bit longer.

3. 赶快 quickly, hurry

   要下雨了，我们赶快走吧。
   It's going to rain, let's go quickly.

   已经八点了，赶快起床吧。
   It's already 8 o'clock. Quick! Get out of bed!

句型与替换练习
(Substitution & Extention)

1. 还有also, in addition

   他会说法语、英语，还有汉语。

   He can speak French, English and Chinese.

   这种衣服的颜色很多，有红色、蓝色，还有黄色。

   This clothing is very colorful, there is red, blue and there is yellow.

   替换例句：

   这里可以买到红茶、绿茶，还有花茶。

   我去过长城、故宫，还有颐和园。

2. 一……就…… indicates that one event follows immediately after the other

   你一到北京，就给我打个电话。

   As soon as you arrive in Beijing, give me a call.

   替换例句：

   你一有消息就马上通知我。

   我打算一放假就去上海。

第 *3* 课

乘出租车
Take A Taxi

课文 (Text)

司机：Nín hǎo, huānyíng lái Běijīng!
司机：您 好， 欢迎 来北京!

Huáng Rénháo: Nín hǎo! Zhè jǐ gè dà xiāngzi jiù fàng zài hòubèixiāng,
黄 人豪：您 好! 这几个大 箱子 就 放 在 后备箱，

xiǎo de jiù suíshēn xiédài ba.
小 的 就 随身 携带 吧。

司机：Xiānsheng, qǐng wèn qù nǎr?
司机：先生， 请 问 去哪儿?

Huáng Rénháo: Míngyuè Fàndiàn.
黄 人豪： 明月 饭店。

司机：Míngyuè Fàndiàn? Zài Yíhéyuán nàr ba?
司机：明月 饭店? 在 颐和园 那儿 吧?

颐和园在北京的西北部，距离机场较远。

Huáng Rénháo: Duì, lí nàli bù yuǎn. Wǒ zhèlǐ yǒu Míngyuè Fàndiàn
黄 人豪：对，离那里不远。我这里有 明月 饭店

de jùtǐ dìzhǐ, nín kànkan.
的 具体 地址，您 看看。

司机：Ō, zhīdao le.
司机：噢，知道 了。

Huáng Rénháo: Běiwǔhuán de rùkǒu, cóng zhèlǐ néng shàng Wǔhuán?
黄 人豪 : 北五环 的 入口，从 这里 能 上 五环？

Xuěméi, nǐ kàn, dōu yǒu Wǔhuánlù le!
雪梅，你 看，都 有 五环路 了！

> 环路，一般是围着城市修建的路。北京现在一共有六条环路。

Xuěméi: Shì a, Běijīng biànhuà zhēn dà.
雪梅：是 啊，北京 变化 真 大。

Sījī : Shì a. Xiànzài dōu yǒu Liùhuánlù le.
司机：是 啊，现在 都 有 六环路 了。

Xiǎojié: Zhèr shì bù shì lí Chángchéng hěn jìn?
小杰：这儿 是 不 是 离 长城 很 近？

Sījī : Méicuòr, cóng zhè ge chūkǒur chūqù jiù néng dào
司机：没错儿，从 这个 出口儿 出去 就能 到

Bādálǐng Chángchéng.
八达岭 长城。

> 八达岭长城，距市区约80公里，是明代长城的代表。

Sījī : Nǐ dì-yī cì lái Běijīng ma?
司机：你 第一 次 来 北京 吗？

Xiǎojié: Zhè shì dì-èr cì. Wǒ hěn xiǎo de shíhou lái guò yī cì.
小杰：这 是 第二 次。我 很 小 的 时候 来过 一 次。

Sījī : Nà nǐ de Hànyǔ shuō de kě zhēn bùcuò.
司机：那 你的 汉语 说得 可 真 不错。

Xiǎojié: Xièxie, wǒ xiànzài zhēngzài xuéxí.

小杰： 谢谢，我 现在 正在 学习。

Sījī : Xiānsheng, nín shì Zhōngguórén?

司机： 先生，您 是 中国人?

Huáng Rénháo: Wǒ zài Zhōngguó chūshēng de, hòulái qù le Měiguó.

黄 人豪： 我 在 中国 出生 的，后来 去 了 美国。

Yǐjīng hǎo jǐ nián méiyǒu huílái le.

已经 好几年 没有 回来 了。

Sījī : Nà nín kě yào hǎohāo kànkan. Zhè jǐ nián biànhuà tài dà le.

司机： 那您可要 好好 看看。这几年 变化 太大了。

Huáng Rénháo: Shì a!

黄 人豪： 是 啊!

Xuěméi: Qǐngwèn, Míngyuè Fàndiàn kuài dào le ma?

雪梅： 请问， 明月 饭店 快 到 了吗?

Sījī : Kuài le, cóng qiánbiān nà gè chūkǒu chūqù, wǎng zuǒ

司机： 快 了，从 前边 那个 出口 出去， 往 左

guǎi, guò le hónglǜdēng jiù dào le.

拐，过了 红绿灯 就到了。

Huáng Rénháo: Xiànzài , zhè zhǒng lìjiāoqiáo hěn duō.

黄 人豪： 现在，这 种 立交桥很 多。

司机：Sījī : Yào wǒ shuō, háishi shǎo. Duō le, jiù bù dǔchē le.
司机：要 我 说，还是 少。多 了，就 不 堵车 了。

Sījī : Dào le.
司机：到 了。

Xuěméi: Duōshao qián?
雪梅：多少 钱？

Sījī : Jiā shàng gāosù gōnglù fèi, yīgòng 96 kuài. Zhǎo nín
司机：加 上 高速 公路 费，一共 96 块。找 您

qián, bié wàng le nín de xíngli.
钱，别 忘 了 您的 行李。

Xuěméi: Xièxie! Zàijiàn!
雪梅：谢谢! 再见!

Sījī : Bùkèqì, zàijiàn!
司机：不客气，再见!

> 在中国乘坐出租车的时候，过路过桥费由乘客支付，但乘客不需要给司机小费。

Driver: Hello! Welcome to Beijing!

Huang Renhao: Hello! Put the big suitcases in the back, we'll carry the smaller ones.

Driver: Sir, where are you going?

Huang Renhao: Mingyue Hotel.

Driver: Mingyue Hotel? Is that around the Summer Palace?

Huang Renhao: That's right. It's not far from there. I have the detailed address for Mingyue Hotel, have a look!

Driver: Oh, I know.

Huang Renhao: Entrance to north fifth ring road! You can get on the fifth ring road from here? Xuemei, there's now a fifth ring road!

Xuemei: Yes, Beijing has changed so much.

Driver: Yes, There's even a sixth ring road now.

Xiaojie: Is this near the Great Wall?

Driver: That's right. Take this exit and you can get to the Badaling Great Wall.

Driver: Is this your first time to Beijing?

Xiaojie: It's my second time. I came here once when I was very young.

Driver: Well, your spoken Chinese is really good.

Xiaojie: Thank you, I'm studying Chinese now.

Driver: Sir, are you Chinese?

Huang Renhao: I was born in China, then I went to the United States. I haven't been back for quite a few years.

Driver: Well, you should take a good look around. There have been so many changes in the past few years.

Huang Renhao: Indeed!

Xuemei: Excuse me, are we near the Mingyue Hotel yet?

Driver: Soon. Just take the exit ahead and make a left turn. The hotel is just past the traffic lights.

Huang Renhao: There are so many fly-overs nowadays.

Driver: There's still not enough, if you ask me. There wouldn't be traffic jams if we had more fly-overs.

Driver: Here we are!

Xuemei: How much is it?

Driver: That's 96 yuan including the freeway toll. Here's your change. Don't forget your luggage!

Xuemei: Thank you! Goodbye!

Driver: You're welcome! Bye!

旅游汉语

生词 (New Words)

1. 司机	sījī	名	driver
2. 欢迎	huānyíng	动	welcome
3. 随身	suíshēn	副	(take) with one
4. 携带	xiédài	动	carry, bring
5. 离	lí	动	leave, part from
6. 具体	jùtǐ	形	concrete, specific
7. 地址	dìzhǐ	名	address, location
8. 噢	ō	叹	oh, aw
9. 知道	zhīdao	动	know
10. 入口	rùkǒu	名	entrance
11. 环路	huánlù	名	ring road
12. 变化	biànhuà	名	change
13. 没错儿	méicuòr	形	correct
14. 第	dì	前缀	used as prefix before a number
15. 时候	shíhou	名	time

16.	汉语	Hànyǔ	名	Chinese
17.	可	kě	副	so, much(emphasis)
18.	出生	chūshēng	动	be born
19.	后来	hòulái	名	later, afterwards
20.	从前	cóngqián	名	before
21.	拐	guǎi	动	turn, change direction
22.	立交桥	lìjiāoqiáo	名	fly-over
23.	堵车	dǔchē	动	traffic jam
24.	高速公路	gāosù gōnglù	名	expressway, freeway
25.	费	fèi	名	fee
26.	别	bié	副	not
27.	忘	wàng	动	forget

注释（Notes）

1. 离

离 indicates "from". 离那里不远。From there, not far. In proper English we'd say "not far from there".

2. 现在都有六环了。

Now there is even a sixth ring road. 都 in this sentence indicates emphasis, like "even", "there is even a sixth ring road".

3. 已经好几年没回来了。

好几年 means "several years", but usually less than ten.

4. 往左拐。

Turn left. 往 indicates towards a certain direction, in this case 左 (left). This word is commonly used in Beijing, other places in China might say 向, which also means "towards". 往左，向左，both mean "towards the left".

5. 要我说，还是少。

要我说 is a colloquial expression, like "if you ask me".

Road in Beijing

Most roads in Beijing follow a strict grid pattern, north, south, east and west, with the exception of the ring roads. These are expressways that circle around the city, like a series of concentric circles.

Before 1949, Beijing was a walled city with nine major gates. In the 1950's, the city wall was replaced with what is now known as the second ring road. This is the major expressway in the middle of the city, which has now expanded far beyond the area of the original, walled city. Until fairly recently, the third ring road roughly marked the limit of the developed urban area. But Beijing has continued to expand at a rapid pace. Now there are fourth, fifth and sixth ring roads. In general, outside of the fourth ring road you will find mainly factories, rural areas and satellite communities.

Funny thing is, there is no first ring road. In my mind, the first ring road should probably be considered the road that follows around the outside of Tian'anmen Square. After all, Tian'anmen Square is the centre of Beijing, but locals never refer to this as the "first ring road".

旅游汉语

语言点（Bookmarks）

1. 离 from

这儿离我们家不太远。

It's not too far to our house from here.

现在离飞机起飞还有十分钟。

From now to the time the plane takes off, there is about 10 minutes.

2. 都 even

他说的话我一句都听不懂。

I can't even understand one word of what he is saying.

你的朋友我一个都不认识。

I don't even know one of your friends.

3. 往 towards

请一直往前走。

Please keep going straight.

过了红绿灯，然后往左拐。

After you pass the traffic light, turn left.

句型与替换练习
（Substitution & Extention）

1. 正在…… indicates something is just happening

我们正在学习汉语。

We are learning Chinese right now.

替换例句：

> 我们正在颐和园呢。
> 外边正在下雨呢。

2. 就……了 indicates that something will happen soon

还有一个小时就到中国了。

We are going to be in China in just one hour.

替换例句：

> 飞机就要起飞了。
> 我的签证就要到期了。

第4课

丢包
Lost Bag

旅游 汉语

课文（Text）

Huáng Rénháo: Zǒu ba, wǒmen jìnqù ba.
黄 人豪：走 吧，我们 进去 吧。

Xiǎojié: Wǒ de nà gè bāo ne?
小杰：我 的 那个 包 呢？

Xuěméi: Nǎ gè?
雪梅：哪 个？

Xiǎojié: Zhuāng zhàoxiàngjī de nà gè bāo.
小杰： 装 照相机 的 那个 包。

Huáng Rénháo: Xià fēijī de shíhou bāo hái zài ne.
黄 人豪：下 飞机 的 时候 包 还 在 呢。

> "落"在这儿不读"luò"，而读"là"，表示"丢"和"漏掉"的意思。丢三落四是指一个人办事不认真，容易丢东西。

Xiǎojié: Duì, nà gè bāo méiyǒu tuōyùn. Wǒ yìzhí suíshēn dàizhe ne!
小杰：对，那个 包 没有 托运。我 一直 随身 带着 呢！

Huáng Rénháo: Nà méizhǔnr là chūzūchē shàng le.
黄 人豪：那 没准儿 落 出租车 上 了。

Xiǎojié: Duì, yīnwèi zuòwèi tài xiǎo, wǒ bǎ xiàngjī fàng zài hòubian le.
小杰：对，因为 座位 太 小，我 把 相机 放在 后边 了。

Xuěméi: Nǐ ya, diūsānlàsì de máobìng yě dài dào Zhōngguó
雪梅：你 呀， 丢三落四 的 毛病 也 带到 中国

lái le.
来 了。

Xiǎojié: Māma, nà lǐbianr hái yǒu pāi wán de jiāojuǎn ne.
小杰：妈妈，那里边儿还有拍完的胶卷呢。

Fúwùyuán: Qǐng wèn, nín yǒu shénme shìqing xūyào bāngmáng ma?
服务员：请问，您有什么事情需要帮忙吗？

Huáng Rénháo: Shì zhèyàng, wǒmen de yī gè bāo kěnéng là zài
黄人豪：是这样，我们的一个包可能落在

gāngcái sòng wǒmen de chūzūchē shàng le.
刚才送我们的出租车上了。

Xiǎojié: Shì yī gè zhuāng zhàoxiàngjī de.
小杰：是一个装照相机的。

Fúwùyuán: Shénmeyàng de chūzūchē? Chēhào nín jìde ma?
服务员：什么样的出租车？车号您记得吗？

Huáng Rénháo: Méiyǒu, nǐmen ne?
黄人豪：没有，你们呢？

Xuě méi: Wǒ zhǐ jìde shì lǜsè de.
雪梅：我只记得是绿色的。

Fúwùyuán: Bié zháojí, nǐmen jìnlái zuò yīhuìr, wǒmen xiǎngxiang bànfǎ.
服务员：别着急，你们进来坐一会儿，我们想想办法。

Xuě méi: Xièxie.
雪梅：谢谢。

Fúwùyuán: Xiānsheng, méi jìzhù chēhào méiguānxi. Nín yǒu chūzūchē
服务员： 先生，没 记住 车号 没关系。您 有 出租车

de fāpiào ma?
的 发票 吗？

Huáng Rénháo: Fāpiào?
黄 人豪： 发票？

出租车发票上都有出租车公司的电话和出租车的车号。

Fúwùyuán: Zhǎo nín qián shí gěi nín de.
服务员： 找 您 钱 时给您 的。

Huáng Rénháo: Shì zhè gè ma?
黄 人豪： 是 这 个 吗？

Fúwùyuán: Duì, jiù shì zhè gè, nín kàn shàngmiàn yǒu chūzūchē
服务员： 对，就 是 这 个，您 看 上面 有 出租车

de diànhuà hàomǎ, hái yǒu chūzūchē de chēhào.
的 电话 号码，还 有 出租车 的 车号。

Xuěméi: Zhème shuō, kěyǐ zhǎodào nà liàng chūzūchē le.
雪梅： 这么 说，可以 找到 那 辆 出租车 了。

Fúwùyuán: Duì, bié zháojí. Wǒmen xiànzài jiù gěi chūzūchē gōngsī
服务员： 对，别 着急。我们 现在 就 给 出租车 公司

dǎ diànhuà.
打 电话。

服务员：喂，您好！我们这儿有 三 位客人，刚才
Fúwùyuán: Wéi, nín hǎo! Wǒmen zhèr yǒu sān wèi kèrén, gāngcái

坐 了 你们 的 车，可能 有 一个 包 落 在 你们
zuò le nǐmen de chē, kěnéng yǒu yī gè bāo là zài nǐmen

车 上 了。车号？您 稍 等 …… 您 跟 他
chē shàng le. Chēhào? Nín shāo děng …… Nín gēn tā

说 一下儿 吧。
shuō yíxiàr ba.

黄 人豪 ：喂，您 好！车号 是 BAF123。对，是 从
Huáng Rénháo: Wéi, nín hǎo! Chēhào shì BAF123. Duì, shì cóng

机场 打 车 到 饭店 的。好，谢谢！
jīchǎng dǎ chē dào fàndiàn de. Hǎo, xièxie!

小杰 ：怎么样？
Xiǎojié: Zěnmeyàng?

黄 人豪 ：他们 得 跟 出租车 司机 联系 一下，有 了 结果
Huáng Rénháo: Tāmen děi gēn chūzūchē sījī liánxì yíxià, yǒu le jiéguǒ

给 我们 打 电话。
gěi wǒmen dǎ diànhuà.

小杰 ：哎，又 得 等！
Xiǎojié: Ài, yòu děi děng!

Huang Renhao: Oh, let's going room.

Xiaojie: Where's my bag?

Xuemei: Which one?

Xiaojie: The one with the camera in it?

Huang Renhao: The bag was still there when we got off the plane.

Xiaojie: That's right, the bag wasn't part of check-in luggage. I've been carrying it with me!

Huang Renhao: Then you probably left it in the taxi.

Xiaojie: Yes, because the seat was so small, I put the camera in the back.

Xuemei: Oh no, you've brought your forgetful habit to China.

Xiaojie: Mom, there is even film in the camera.

Staff: Excuse me, do you need help with anything?

Huang Renhao: It's like this, one of our bags may have been left behind in our taxi just now.

Xiaojie: It's a camera bag.

Staff: What sort of taxi? Do you remember the taxi number?

Huang Renhao: No, do you remember?

Xuemei: I only remember it was green.

Staff: Don't panic, come in and sit down, we'll think of something.

Xuemei: Thank you!

Staff: Sir, it's alright if you don't remember the taxi number. You still have the taxi receipt, right?

Huang Renhao: The receipt?

Staff: It was given to you with the change.

Huang Renhao: Is this the one?

Staff: This is it. You see, the receipt has the phone number of the taxi company, as well as the taxi's number plates.

Xuemei: This means we can find that taxi.

Staff: Yes, don't worry. We'll give the taxi company a call right now.

Staff: Hello! It's Mingyue Hotel here. We have three guests who just arrived in one of your taxis. They may have left a bag in the taxi. The number of the taxi? Wait a moment, please. You'd better talk to him.

Huang Renhao: Hello. The number plates are BAF123. Yes, from the airport to the hotel. Great, thanks!

Xiaojie: What's happening?

Huang Renhao: They need to contact the taxi driver. They'll call us once they know something.

Xiaojie: Now we have to wait again!

旅游汉语

生词（New Words）

1. 照相机	zhàoxiàngjī	名	camera
2. 一直	yīzhí	副	all along
3. 落	là	动	lose
4. 丢三落四	diūsānlàsì		forgetful
5. 毛病	máobìng	名	bad habit
6. 拍	pāi	动	take (pictures)
7. 胶卷	jiāojuǎn	名	roll of camera film
8. 服务员	fúwùyuán	名	service staff
9. 事情	shìqing	名	thing
10. 需要	xūyào	动	need
11. 帮忙	bāngmáng	动	help
12. 刚才	gāngcái	名	(just) a moment ago
13. 记得	jìde	动	remember
14. 着急	zháojí	形	get worried
15. 办法	bànfǎ	名	method

16. 发票	fāpiào	名	receipt, invoice
17. 找钱	zhǎoqián		make change
18. 辆	liàng	量	measure word for vehicles
19. 打车	dǎchē		take taxi
20. 客人	kèrén	名	guest
21. 稍	shāo	副	a little

注释（Notes）

1. 我一直随身带着。

I carried it with me the whole time. 一直 means "all the way", or "the whole time, for the whole duration".

2. 我把相机放在后边了。

I put the camera behind me. This kind of sentence structure using 把 is very common. It's a way of putting the object before the verb. We don't usually do that in English. We would say "I put the camera behind me". But to translate directly, 我把相机放在后边了. I 把 the camera put behind me.

3. 丢三落四的毛病也带到中国来了。

You've brought your habit of losing things all the way to China. 丢 and 落 both mean "to lose", or "leave something behind". 丢三落四 literally means "lose threes and fours". This is just a way of saying that you lose all kinds of things. Note that the character 落 is also pronounced luò, but here it should be là.

4. 可能落在刚才送我们的出租车上了。

Perhaps we left it in the taxi that just brought us here. Remember, 落 means "to leave something by accident, to lose it".

5. 找您钱时给您的。

It was given to you with the change. 找钱 is to make change.

文化背景（Sign Posts）

Taxis in Beijing

Taking a taxi in Beijing is relatively straightforward. Taxis are clearly marked, with roof lights as well as special paint jobs. Different companies sometimes use different colours. Regardless, a legitimate taxi should be clearly marked, and have an official, working meter.

You should never have to negotiate the price of a taxi trip. Instead, you should insist on "走表" (use the meter). The only exception is if you are going to be travelling far out of the urban area, or reserving the car for a whole day. For example, if you take a taxi all the way to the Great Wall, you might negotiate a flat fare in advance.

There is no tipping for taxis. You simply pay the fare listed on the meter, and you should be given a printed receipt. The only extra charges are for road tolls, like on the airport expressway. Even then, you should be given the receipt that shows the exact amount of the toll.

If you ever have a problem with a taxi, just write down the taxi number that is listed on the inside and the outside of the car. Taxis are very strictly regulated, and all complaints are taken seriously. In fact, if the driver sees you writing down the number, that's usually enough to solve any problem right away.

In my experience, the vast majority of taxi drivers are honest and hard-working. It's a very tough job.

语言点（Bookmarks）

1. 一直 all along

这几天，天气一直都很冷。

These few days, the weather has been cold all the way through.

过了十字路口一直往南走。

After you pass the intersection, keep going south.

2. 落 to lose something

书包落在车上了。

The book bag was lost in the car.

下车前，好好看看，别落东西。

When you get out of the car, take a good look around. Don't forget anything.

3. 记得 remember

你记得出租车的车号吗?

Do you remember the car number of the taxi?

我不记得他的电话号码了。

I don't remember his telephone number anymore.

4. 得 must, have to

坐车去机场得40分钟。

It will take 40 minutes to get to the airport by car.

买这件衣服得花不少钱。

It will take a lot of money to buy this clothing.

旅游汉语

句型与替换练习
(Substitution & Extention)

1. 把 a way of putting the object in front of the verb

　　S＋把＋O＋V＋ (something else)

　　你把护照给我看看。

　　Show me your passport.

　　他把饭店的杯子打碎了。

　　He broke the hotel glass.

　　Tips:

- Not all verbs can be used in this sentence structure.
- Something else must follow the verb, or it could be a double verb.

替换例句：

　　请帮我把行李送到楼上去。

　　请把照相机递给我。

入住
Check In

旅游汉语

课文 (Text)

Huáng Rénháo:　Wǒmen yào bànlǐ rùzhù.
黄　人豪：我们 要 办理 入住。

Fúwùyuán:　Qǐng wèn yùdìng fángjiān le ma?
服务员：请 问 预订 房间 了 吗?

Huáng Rénháo:　Yùdìng le.
黄　人豪：预订 了。

Fúwùyuán:　Nín shuō yíxiàr xìngmíng.
服务员：您 说 一下儿 姓名。

Huáng Rénháo:　Huáng Rénháo, Měiguó Niǔyuē lái de.
黄　人豪：黄　人豪，美国 纽约 来 的。

Fúwùyuán:　Nín yùdìng le liǎng gè fángjiān, yī gè shuāngrénjiān,
服务员：您 预订 了 两 个 房间，一 个 双人间，

yī gè dānjiān.
一 个 单间。

Huáng Rénháo:　Duì!
黄　人豪：对!

Fúwùyuán:　Qǐng gěi wǒ kàn yíxiàr nǐmen de hùzhào. Xièxie.
服务员：请 给 我 看 一下儿 你们 的 护照。谢谢。

Máfan nín zài tián yīxiàr rù zhù dēngjì dān.

麻烦 您 再 填 一下儿 入 住 登记 单。

Huáng Rénháo: Hǎo.

黄 人豪 : 好。

Fúwùyuán: Xièxie. Qǐng jiāo yīxiàr yùfùkuǎn.

服务员 : 谢谢。请 交 一下儿 预付款。

Xuěméi: Néng shuā kǎ ma?

雪梅 : 能 刷卡 吗?

Fúwùyuán: Kěyǐde. Hǎode, xièxie. Zhè shì nǐmen de fángkǎ,

服务员 : 可以的。好的,谢谢。这 是 你们 的 房卡,

liǎng jiān fáng: yī gè shì 1183, yī gè shì 1179.

两 间 房:一 个 是 1183,一 个 是 1179。

Xuěméi: Zài jǐ céng?

雪梅 : 在 几 层?

Fúwùyuán: Dōu zài 11 céng.

服务员 : 都 在 11 层。

Xuěméi: Nà gè shuāngrénjiān shì cháo nán de ma?

雪梅 : 那个 双人间 是 朝 南 的 吗?

Fúwùyuán: 1183 bù shì, cháo xī.

服务员 : 1183 不 是, 朝 西。

Xuěméi: Néng bù néng bǎ shuāngrénjiān huàn chéng cháo nán
雪梅： 能 不 能 把 双人间 换 成 朝 南

de ne? Wǒ xǐhuan cháo nán de fángjiān.
的 呢？我 喜欢 朝 南 的 房间。

Huáng Rénháo: Duì, wǒmen zài zhèlǐ yào zhù yī gè xīngqī zuǒyòu,
黄 人豪 ： 对，我们 在 这里 要 住 一个 星期 左右，

qǐng bāng wǒmen huàn yīxiàr.
请 帮 我们 换 一下儿。

Fúwùyuán: Wǒ cháyīchá yǒu méi yǒu kòng fángjiān. Hái yǒu yī jiān,
服务员： 我 查一查 有 没 有 空 房间。还 有 一间，

bùguò bù shì zài 11 céng.
不过 不 是 在 11 层。

Xuěméi: Méiguānxi, zài jǐ céng?
雪梅： 没关系，在 几 层？

Fúwùyuán: 9 céng, 918 fáng.
服务员： 9 层，918 房。

Xuěméi: Wǒ jiù yào 918 fángjiān.
雪梅： 我 就 要 918 房间。

Fúwùyuán: Cāntīng zài èr céng, yī céng de zuǒbian yǒu yī gè
服务员： 餐厅 在 二层，一 层 的 左边 有 一个

kāfēitīng.

咖啡厅。

Fúwùyuán: Tāmen huì bāng nǐmen bǎ xíngli nádào fángjiān.

服务员：他们 会 帮 你们 把 行李 拿到 房间。

Huáng Rénháo: Hǎo. Xièxie! Wǒmen zǒu. Ài, Xiǎojié ne?

黄 人豪：好。谢谢！我们 走。哎，小杰 呢？

Xuěméi: Ō, zài zhèr ne! Xiǎojié, let's go!

雪梅：噢，在 这儿 呢! 小杰，let's go!

Xíngli gōng: Zhè shì nín de fángjiān.

行李工：这是 您的 房间。

Xuěméi: Xièxie nín!

雪梅：谢谢 您!

Xíngli gōng: Xièxie, wǒmen bù shōu xiǎofèi, zàijiàn.

行李工：谢谢，我们 不 收 小费，再见。

Xuěméi: Wǒ wàng le, Zhōngguó bù shōu xiǎofèi.

雪梅：我 忘 了，中国 不 收 小费。

Huáng Rénháo: Zǒu, wǒmen qù Xiǎojié de fángjiān kànkan.

黄 人豪：走，我们 去 小杰 的 房间 看看。

Xuěméi: Zǒu ba.

雪梅：走 吧。

Huang Renhao: We'd like to check in.

Staff: Have you made room reservations?

Huang Renhao: Yes, we have.

Staff: Please tell me the name.

Huang Renhao: Huang Renhao, from New York, the United States.

Staff: You reserved two rooms, a double and a single.

Huang Renhao: That's right!

Staff: Please show me your passports. Thank you. Then fill in a registration card.

Huang Renhao: OK.

Staff: Thank you! Please pay the deposit.

Xuemei: Do you take credit cards?

Staff: Yes. Thank you! These are your room keycards, one room is 1183, the other is 1179.

Xuemei: Which floor are they on?

Staff: They're both on the 11th floor.

Xuemei: Is the double room facing south?

Staff: No, 1183 faces west.

Xuemei: Can you change the double room to a south-facing one? I like south-facing rooms.

Huang Renhao: We'll be staying here for about a week, please change the room for us.

Staff: I'll check to see if there are any vacant rooms. Yes, there's one, but it's not on the 11th floor.

Xuemei: That's alright, which floor is it on?

Staff: 9th floor, room 918.

Xuemei: We'll take room 918.

Staff: The restaurant is on the 2nd floor, there's a café to the left on the 1st floor.

Staff: They will take the luggage to your room.

Huang Renhao: Thank you! Let's go. Where is Xiaojie?

Xuemei: Here she is. Xiaojie, let's go!

Porter: This is your room.

Xuemei: Thank you!

Porter: Thanks, but we can't accept that. Goodbye!

Xuemei: I forgot, you don't need to tip in China.

Huang Renhao: Let's go have a look at Xiaojie's room.

Xuemei: Let's go.

旅游汉语

生词（New Words）

1. 办理	bànlǐ	动	handle
2. 入住	rùzhù	动	check in
3. 预订	yùdìng	动	subscribe
4. 姓名	xìngmíng	名	family name and given name
5. 登记卡	dēngjìkǎ	名	register card
6. 交	jiāo	动	hand in
7. 预付款	yùfùkuǎn	名	advanced payment
8. 刷卡	shuākǎ		take credit card
9. 层	céng	量	measure word for layers
10. 朝	cháo	介	facing
11. 换	huàn	动	change
12. 左右	zuǒyòu	名	about
13. 不过	búguò	连	but
14. 餐厅	cāntīng	名	dining hall
15. 咖啡厅	kāfēitīng	名	café

16. 小费	xiǎofèi	名	tip

专有名词 (Proper Noun)

纽约	Niǔyuē		New York

旅游汉语

注释（Notes）

1. 我们要办理入住。

入 means to enter, 住 is to live. So, 入住 is to check into a hotel.

2. 请说一下儿姓名。

说一下儿 is a softer, more polite way of asking for information. Instead of simply saying 姓名 name, 请说一下儿姓名 is more like "please tell me your name". 姓名 actually means your surname 姓 and given name 名字. 姓名 means your whole name. In Beijing we often come across the 儿 ending. Instead of 请说一下, the clerk says 请说一下儿. Sometimes the 儿 ending is required, often it is optional. In this phrase, it's optional, but very commonly used in Beijing.

3. 能不能把双人间换成朝南的房间？

Would it be possible to exchange the double room for a room that faces south? 能不能 means "would it be possible".

4. 我们在这里要住一个星期左右。

We're going to stay here for about a week. 左 means left, 右 means right, put together, 左右 means approximately. It might not matter for a day or two, but since they will be staying here a week or more, it would be nice to have their preference.

文化背景（Sign Posts）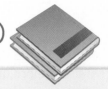

Hotels in China (1)

There are several different words for hotel. "饭店" is the most common term, but sometimes this word is also used for restaurants. "宾馆", guesthouse, is also common, as is "大酒楼" or "大酒店". Note that although they use the word "酒", wine, these shouldn't be translated as "great wine building". This is just one of those terms that has been passed down, and changed meanings over time. "饭店" and "大酒店" are usually large, fancy hotels. "宾馆" could be large or small. "旅馆" guesthouse, would be smaller and more inexpensive. "招待所" are often guesthouses that belong to a certain government department, large company or factory. Sometimes these are for internal use only.

"涉外宾馆" or "涉外饭店" are terms to describe hotels that are mainly for foreign tourists. "涉" is to involve, or relate to. "涉外", concerning foreign affairs. Most tourist hotels take both Chinese and foreign nationals nowadays, but sometimes the cheapest, lowest quality accommodations do not have a license that permits them to take foreign tourists.

As for tipping, this is sometimes accepted in China, but much more rarely than in the West. Taxis, for example, do not expect a tip. Nor do you leave a tip in a restaurant. In the tourism industry, many businesses like hotels and fancy restaurants will charge a service fee, usually 15%. In this case, you certainly don't need to leave a tip.

If you do choose to give a tip, it won't always be refused. But it is your own choice and, in the vast majority of situations, is not expected.

语言点 （Bookmarks）

1. 能 to be able to

您能给我看一下儿您的护照吗？

Could you show me your passport for a moment?

您现在不能换房间。

You can't change rooms now.

2. 都 all

这些都是我们的行李。

This luggage is all ours.

我们都是从美国来的。

We are all from the United States.

3. 左右 approximately

一个双人间一天大概300块钱左右。

One double room per day is approximately 300 *yuan*.

他大概50岁左右。

He is around 50 years old.

4. 不过 but

这个房间不错，不过小了一点儿。

This room is not bad, but it's a little small.

北京的秋天天气很好，不过空气很干燥。

The weather in the autumn in Beijing is quite nice, but the air is a little bit dry.

旅游汉语

句型与替换练习
(Substitution & Extention)

1. 一下儿 a polite, colloquial expression

   我来介绍一下儿，这是我的朋友。

   Let me make a brief introduction. This is my friend.

   替换例句：

   请等一下儿，好吗?

   我想打听一下儿，怎么去银行?

第 6 课

在房间
In The Room

旅游汉语

课文（Text）

Xuěméi: Xiǎojié, fángjiān zěnmeyàng?
雪梅：小杰，房间　怎么样？

Xiǎojié: Tǐng hǎo de. Zhàoxiàngjī, zěnme hái méi yǒu xiāoxi ne?
小杰：挺　好　的。照相机，怎么　还没　有　消息　呢？

Huáng Rénháo: Bié zháojí, wǒ yǐjīng tōngzhī fúwùtái le, yǒu xiāoxi
黄　人豪：别　着急，我　已经　通知　服务台　了，有　消息

tāmen mǎshàng huì gàosu zánmen de.
他们　马上　会　告诉　咱们　的。

Xuěméi: Yǐhòu yào zhàogù hǎo zìjǐ de dōngxi a.
雪梅：以后　要　照顾　好　自己的　东西　啊。

Huáng Rénháo: Kànkan diànshì jiémù ba, kànkan Zhōngguó de diànshì
黄　人豪：看看　电视　节目　吧，看看　　中国　的　电视

jiémù.
节目。

Xiǎojié: Yǒu Měiguó de diànshì jiémù ma?
小杰：有　美国　的　电视　节目　吗？

Huáng Rénháo: Wǒ wènwen.
黄　人豪：我　问问。

Huáng Rénháo: Nín hǎo, shì qiántái ma? Qǐngwèn, fángjiān lǐ de diànshì
黄　人豪：您好，是 前台 吗？请问，房间 里的 电视

néng kàndào Měiguó de diànshì píndào ma? Nà nǎ gè
能　看到 美国 的 电视 频道 吗？那 哪个

píndào kěyǐ kàndào tǐyù jiémù ne?
频道 可以 看到 体育 节目 呢？

Huáng Rénháo: Duìbuqǐ, wǒ méiyǒu zhǎodào tǐyù píndào. Hǎo, xièxie.
黄　人豪：对不起，我 没有 找到 体育 频道。好，谢谢。

Tā shuō shànglái gěi zánmen tiáoshì yīxiàr.
她说 上来 给 咱们 调试 一下儿。

Fúwùyuán: Nín hǎo, wǒ bāng nín tiáo shì yīxiàr.
服务员：您好，我帮 您 调试 一下儿。

Huáng Rénháo: Hǎo de.
黄　人豪：好的。

Fúwùyuán: Zhè shì tǐyù píndào, zhè shì Yīngyǔ píndào.
服务员：这 是 体育 频道，这 是 英语 频道。

Fúwùyuán: Ō, duì le, bīngxiāng lǐ háiyǒu yǐnliào hé píjiǔ.
服务员：噢，对 了，冰箱 里 还有 饮料和 啤酒。

Xuěméi: Ài, wǒ yǒu gè wèntí xiǎng wèn nǐ, fángjiān néng dǎ
雪梅：唉，我 有 个 问题 想 问 你，房间 能 打

guónèi chángtúdiànhuà ma?
国内 长途电话 吗？

Fúwùyuán: Duìbuqǐ, xiànzài hái bù néng, zhǐ néng dǎ shìnèi diànhuà.
服务员：对不起，现在还不能，只能 打市内 电话。

Xuěméi: Yàoshi dǎ guónèi chángtú de huà, zěnme bàn ne?
雪梅：要是打 国内 长途的话，怎么 办 呢?

Fúwùyuán: Nín xūyào dào fúwùtái bànlǐ kāitōng shǒuxù, kāitōng
服务员：您 需要到 服务台 办理 开通 手续，开通

yǐhòu jiù kěyǐ dǎ le.
以后 就 可以 打 了。

Xuěméi: Guójì chángtú néng dǎ ma?
雪梅：国际 长途 能 打吗?

Fúwùyuán: Dǎ guójì chángtú xūyào dào fúwùtái bànlǐ yājīn shǒuxù,
服务员：打 国际 长途 需要 到 服务台 办理 押金 手续，

ránhòu jiù kěyǐ dǎ le.
然后 就 可以 打 了。

Xuěméi: Shì zhèyàng, míngbai le.
雪梅：是 这样， 明白 了。

Huáng Rénháo: Wǒmen chūqù chī diǎnr fàn ba. Qìngzhù yīxiàr.
黄 人豪：我们 出去 吃 点儿 饭 吧。庆祝 一下儿。

Xuěméi: Hǎo a, Xiǎojié, zánmen zǒu ba.
雪梅：好 啊，小杰，咱们 走 吧。

Xiǎojié: Nǐmen qù ba,   wǒ bù xiǎng qù le.
小杰：你们 去 吧，我 不 想 去 了。

Huáng Rénháo: Wéi,   nǐ hǎo! Shénme! Zhàoxiàngjī bāo,   yǐjīng gěi
黄 人豪：喂，你 好！什么！ 照相机 包，已经 给

wǒmen sònglái le.   Xièxie!
我们 送来 了。谢谢！

Xiǎojié: Wǒ de zhàoxiàngjī huílái le.
小杰：我 的 照相机 回来 了。

Huáng Rénháo: Shì a.
黄 人豪：是 啊。

Xiǎojié: Bàba、māma, zánmen qù chīfàn ba, wǒ kě zhēn è le.
小杰：爸爸、妈妈，咱们 去 吃饭 吧，我 可 真 饿了。

Huáng Rénháo: Hǎo, zǒu!
黄 人豪：好，走！

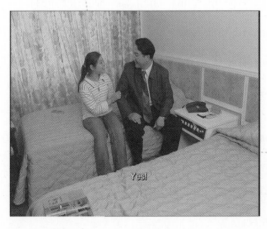

Xuemei: Xiaojie, how's your room?

Xiaojie: It's alright. How come there's no news about the camera yet?

Huang Renhao: Don't worry, I've already told reception. They'll let us know as soon as there's news.

Xuemei: You've got to look after your belongings from now on!

Huang Renhao: Watch some TV, see what's showing on Chinese television.

Xiaojie: Are there any American programmes?

Huang Renhao: Let me ask.

Huang Renhao: Hello. Is it front desk? Could you tell me if the TV in the room can get American channels? Well, which channel is for sports programmes?

Huang Renhao: Sorry, I can't find the sports channel. OK, thanks! She said she would send someone to tune it.

Staff: Let me tune it for you.

Huang Renhao: Thank you!

Staff: This is the sports channel, and this is the English channel.

Staff: Oh, that's right, there are drinks and beer in the fridge.

Xuemei: I want to ask you a question. Can the phones in the room make national long distance calls?

Staff: Sorry, that's not available yet, you can only make local calls.

Xuemei: Then how do we make national long distance calls?

Staff: You'll need to apply the service at reception, then you can make the calls.

Xuemei: Can you make international calls?

Staff: For international long distance calls you need to pay a deposit at reception. Then you can make the calls.

Xuemei: Now I understand.

Huang Renhao: Let's go get something to eat. Celebrate a bit.

Xuemei: Good ideas. Xiaojie, let's go?

Xiaojie: You guys go, I don't want to go.

Huang Renhao: Hello! What! They've already sent the camera bag back. Thank you!

Xiaojie: I've got my camera back.

Huang Renhao: Yes.

Xiaojie: Dad, Mom. Let's go and eat. I'm really hungry.

Huang Renhao: OK! Let's go.

旅游汉语

 生词（New Words）

1. 挺	tǐng	副	very
2. 消息	xiāoxi	名	news
3. 马上	mǎshàng	副	at once
4. 以后	yǐhòu	名	after
5. 照顾	zhàogù	动	look after
6. 电视	diànshì	名	TV
7. 频道	píndào	名	channel
8. 体育	tǐyù	名	sports
9. 节目	jiémù	名	programme
10. 调试	tiáoshì	动	tune
11. 冰箱	bīngxiāng	名	refrigerator
12. 饮料	yǐnliào	名	beverage
13. 啤酒	píjiǔ	名	beer
14. 长途	chángtú	形	long distance
15. 要是	yàoshi	连	if

16. ……的话	...de huà		if
17. 手续	shǒuxù	名	procedures
18. 国际	guójì	名	international
19. 押金	yājīn	名	deposit
20. 然后	ránhòu	连	then
21. 庆祝	qìngzhù	动	celebrate
22. 饿	è	形	hungry

旅游汉语

注释（Notes）

1. 小杰,你的房间怎么样?

What is your room like, Xiaojie? 怎么样? What do you think? How about that? 怎么样 is a very common form of question, simply asking for someone's reaction or thoughts, or asking about the current situation. Sometimes it's used like the English expressions, what's up, or what do you say?

2. 噢，对了，冰箱里有饮料和啤酒。

Oh, that's right, there are drinks and beer in the fridge. 对了 literally means correct, but here it is used as a colloquial expression to show that the person just remembered something. 哦，对了。 In English we might say "oh, that's right", or "oh, one more thing".

3. 要是打国内长途的话，怎么办呢?

The pattern "要是 something 的话" means if something happens. If I want to make a domestic long distance call, what do I do?

4. 咱们去吃饭吧，我可真饿了。

Let's go and eat, I'm really hungry. 我饿了。 I'm hungry. 我可真饿了。 I am really hungry, I'm starving!

文化背景 （Sign Posts）

Television in China

In many hotels in China you can watch international English satellite channels like CNN and BBC, or even HBO. Hong Kong satellite channels like Phoenix TV and Channel V are even more common. These channels are both in Mandarin Chinese. Phoenix TV is a general purpose channel, Channel V is for music videos. There are others as well, like the Star Movie channel.

Even without these international stations, most hotels will receive 20 or 30 domestic Chinese channels, including both national and regional satellite channels. Most provinces in China have their own local channels as well as one or more satellite channels that can be received throughout China. Watching the local channels is a great way to practice your language skills and learn a little bit about what's happening in the area you are visiting. Many cities even have their own channels that can be received locally.

The national broadcaster, China Central Television or CCTV, has over a dozen channels. Right now you're watching CCTV-9, the English channel (英语频道). There are also special channels for sports, movies, television dramas, news, children's programming, even traditional arts like Peking Opera. Viewers outside of China will be most familiar with CCTV-9 and CCTV-4, the Chinese language international channel, as these are both relayed by satellite to cover almost the whole world. CCTV-1 and CCTV-2 are mostly general channels, especially focusing on news and current affairs. No matter where you are in China, even in the most remote areas, you can almost always receive CCTV-1.

语言点（Bookmarks）

1. 怎么样 a general question like "what do you think?" or "what's up?"

你觉得北京的天气怎么样?

What do you think about the weather in Beijing?

六点了，一起去吃晚饭怎么样?

It's 6 o'clock. Why don't we go for dinner together?

2. 别 don't

今天天气不好，我们别出去了。

The weather is no good today. Let's not go out.

时间太晚了，别看电视了。

It's too late. Don't watch TV anymore.

旅游汉语

句型与替换练习
(Substitution & Extention)

1. ……的话（要是……的话，如果……的话）indicates a hypothesis

要是方便的话，请给我打个电话。

If it's convenient, please give me a phone call.

如果有时间的话，我们今天下午就去颐和园。

If we have time, we can go to the Summer Palace this afternoon.

替换例句：

你要是去书店的话，请帮我买一张地图。

如果你现在有事的话，那我明天再来。

2. 可……了 to show emphasis

她的汉语说得可好了。

Her Chinese is really quite good.

替换例句：

王府井的人可多了。

北京的冬天可冷了。

打电话
Give A Call

旅游汉语

课文 (Text)

Xuěméi: Ài, zánmen yīnggāi gěi biǎojiě hé Shànghǎi de shūshu
雪梅： 哎，咱们 应该 给 表姐 和 上海 的 叔叔

dǎ gè diànhuà.
打 个 电话。

Huáng Rénháo: Wǒ yě zhèng xiǎng zhe zhè jiàn shìr ne.
黄 人豪： 我 也 正 想 着 这 件 事儿 呢。

Xuěméi: Bù zhīdào zánmen xíngli yǒu méiyǒu xiāoxi.
雪梅： 不 知道 咱们 行李 有 没有 消息。

Huáng Rénháo: Zhènghǎo dǎ diànhuà wènwen biǎojiě.
黄 人豪： 正好 打 电话 问问 表姐。

Xuěméi: Yòng zánmen fángjiān de diànhuà jiù kěyǐ dǎ shìnèi diànhuà.
雪梅： 用 咱们 房间 的 电话 就 可以 打 市内 电话。

Huáng Rénháo: Xiān bō 0, ránhòu bō diànhuà hàomǎ.
黄 人豪： 先 拨 0，然后 拨 电话 号码。

Xuěméi: 0 - 45687425， tōng le.
雪梅： 0—45687425，通 了。

Huáng Rénháo: Wéi, wǒ shì Rénháo a.
黄 人豪： 喂，我 是 人豪 啊。

Biǎojiě: Rénháo, nǐmen zěnmeyàng? Zhù zài nǎli a?
表姐： 人豪，你们 怎么样？ 住 在 哪里 啊？

Huáng Rénháo: Tǐng shùnlì de, wǒmen zhù zài Míngyuè Dàjiǔdiàn.
黄 人豪： 挺 顺利 的，我们 住 在 明月 大酒店。

表姐： 明月　饭店，离我们　家不太　远。行李
Biǎojiě: Míngyuè Fàndiàn,　lí wǒmen jiā bù tài yuǎn. Xíngli

还是　没有　消息？
háishi méiyǒu xiāoxi?

黄　人豪 ： 还 没有 消息。
Huáng Rénháo: Hái méiyǒu xiāoxi.

表姐： 我　明天　想　去　看看 你们，你们 有 没有
Biǎojiě: Wǒ míngtiān xiǎng qù kànkan nǐmen, nǐmen yǒu méiyǒu

时间？
shíjiān?

黄　人豪 ： 明天　下午　怎么样?
Huáng Rénháo: Míngtiān xiàwǔ zěnmeyàng?

表姐： 嗯，好，没问题，就 这么　定 了。
Biǎojiě: Èng, hǎo, méi wèntí, jiù zhème dìng le.

黄　人豪 ： 明天　晚上　我们 一起 吃 晚饭，带 刘 勇
Huáng Rénháo: Míngtiān wǎnshang wǒmen yīqǐ chī wǎnfàn, dài Liú Yǒng

一起 来 吧。我们　好多 年　没 见 了。
yīqǐ lái ba. Wǒmen hǎoduō nián méi jiàn le.

表姐： 那 好 啊，　你们 住 多少　号 房间?
Biǎojiě: Nà hǎo a,　nǐmen zhù duōshao hào fángjiān?

黄　人豪 ： 是 918 房间，　电话　号码 是 总机 转 918
Huáng Rénháo: Shì 918 fángjiān, diànhuà hàomǎ shì zǒngjī zhuǎn 918

房间。总机　电话 的 号码 是 96452626。
fángjiān. Zǒngjī diànhuà de hàomǎ shì 96452626.

Biǎojiě: Hǎo, wǒ jìzhù le, míngtiān jiàn!

表姐：好，我 记住 了，明天 见!

Huáng Rénháo: Xíngli hái méiyǒu xiāoxi. Míngtiān biǎojiě lái.

黄 人豪：行李 还 没有 消息。明天 表姐 来。

Xuěméi: Tài hǎo le, hǎoduō nián méi jiàn tā le.

雪梅：太好了，好多 年 没 见 她 了。

Huáng Rénháo: Gěi Shànghǎi dǎ diànhuà.

黄 人豪：给 上海 打 电话。

Xuěméi: Zánmen fángjiān de diànhuà bù néng dǎ chángtú diànhuà.

雪梅：咱们 房间 的 电话 不能 打 长途 电话。

Huáng Rénháo: Zánmen xiàqù wènwen.

黄 人豪： 咱们 下去 问问。

Qiántái: Nín hǎo!

前台：您 好!

Huáng Rénháo: Nín hǎo! Wǒmen xiǎng wǎng Shànghǎi dǎ diànhuà.

黄 人豪：您 好! 我们 想 往 上海 打 电话，

zěnme bàn bǐjiào hǎo?

怎么 办 比较 好?

Qiántái: Nímen kěyǐ kāitōng nín fángjiān nèi diànhuà de guónèi chángtú,

前台：你们 可以 开通 您 房间 内 电话 的 国内 长途，

zhèyàng nín jiù kěyǐ zài fángjiān nèi zhíjiē dǎ chángtú diànhuà le.

这样 您就 可以 在 房间 内直接 打 长途 电话 了。

Xuěméi: Hái yǒu biéde bànfǎ ma?

雪梅：还 有 别的 办法 吗?

Qiántái: Nín yě kěyǐ mǎi chángtú diànhuàkǎ, zhèyàng nín zài

前台：您 也 可以 买 长途 电话卡，这样 您 在

gōngyòng diànhuà shàng dōu kěyǐ dǎ chángtú diànhuà.

公用 电话 上 都 可以 打 长途 电话。

Huáng Rénháo: Diànhuàkǎ duōshao qián?

黄 人豪 ： 电话卡 多少 钱?

Qiántái: Yǒu 30 kuài, 50 kuài, 100 kuài sān zhǒng.

前台：有 30块、50块、100块 三 种。

Huáng Rénháo: Mǎi 50 kuài de ba.

黄 人豪 ： 买 50块 的 吧。

Qiántái: Hǎo de. Gěi nín.

前台：好 的。给 您。

Xuěméi: Zěnme dǎ Shànghǎi chángtú ne?

雪梅： 怎么 打 上海 长途 呢?

Qiántái: Xiān bō Shànghǎi de qūhào, Shànghǎi de qūhào shì 021,

前台：先 拨 上海 的 区号，上海 的 区号 是 021,

jiē zhe bō diànhuà hàomǎ.

接着 拨 电话 号码。

Huáng Rénháo: Xiè xie

黄 人豪 ： 谢谢。

Qiántái: Bù kè qi.

前台：不 客气。

Xuemei: We should give my cousin and uncle in Shanghai a call.

Huang Renhao: I was just thinking about that too.

Xuemei: I don't know if there's news about the luggage.

Huang Renhao: Just as well we could ask our cousin.

Xuemei: We can make local calls from the phone in our room.

Huang Renhao: Dial zero first, then the phone number.

Xuemei: 0-45687425, it's ringing.

Huang Renhao: Hello, it's Huang Renhao.

Cousin: Renhao, how are you guys? Where are you staying?

Huang Renhao: Everything's fine, we're staying at the Mingyue Hotel.

Cousin: Mingyue Hotel, that's not too far from our place. But there's no news about the luggage?

Huang Renhao: No news yet.

Cousin: I'd love to come see you tomorrow, are you free?

Huang Renhao: How does tomorrow afternoon sound?

Cousin: Sure, that's fine with me. That's settled then.

Huang Renhao: Let's have dinner together tomorrow night, bring Liu Yong with you. We haven't seen each other for years.

Cousin:	Great, which room are you in?
Huang Renhao:	Room 918, just call the switch then ask for extension 918. The hotel switchboard number is 96452626.
Cousin:	I've got it, see you tomorrow!
Huang Renhao:	Still no news on the luggage. My cousin is coming tomorrow.
Xuemei:	That's wonderful, we haven't seen here in so many years.
Huang Renhao:	Make a call to Shanghai.
Xuemei:	You can't make long distance calls from the phone in our room.
Huang Renhao:	Let's go down and ask.
Reception:	Hello.
Huang Renhao:	Hello. We'd like to call Shanghai. What's the best way to do that?
Reception:	You can apply the long distance call service. Then you can make long distance calls in your room.
Xuemei:	Are there any other ways?
Reception:	You can also buy a phone card that works on all these public phones.
Huang Renhao:	How much does a phone card cost?
Reception:	There are three types of cards that cost 30 *yuan*, 50 *yuan* or 100 *yuan* each.
Huang Renhao:	I'll buy a 50 *yuan* card.
Reception:	OK. Here you are.
Xuemei:	How do we make long distance calls to Shanghai?
Reception:	Dial Shanghai's area code first, it's 021, then dial the number.
Huang Renhao:	Thank you!
Reception:	My pleasure.

旅游汉语

生词 （New Words）

1. 叔叔	shūshu	名	uncle
2. 正好	zhènghǎo	副	happen to
3. 拨	bō	动	dial
4. 通	tōng	动	connect
5. 顺利	shùnlì	形	smooth
6. 一起	yìqǐ	副	together
7. 总机	zǒngjī	名	switch board
8. 比较	bǐjiào	副	comparatively
9. 直接	zhíjiē	副	directly
10. 买	mǎi	动	buy
11. 公用	gōngyòng	形	public
12. 区号	qūhào	名	area code

专有名词 (Proper Nouns)

1. 上海	Shànghǎi		Shanghai
2. 刘勇	Liú Yǒng		Liu Yong

注释 (Notes)

1. 正好打电话问问表姐。

正好 indicates a convenient coincidence. In other words, while we're calling the relatives to let them know we've arrived, let's ask about the luggage.

2. 先拨0，然后拨电话号码。

First dial zero, then dial the telephone number.

3. 我明天想去看看你们。

Tomorrow I'd like to go and visit you. When a verb is repeated this way, 看看, it indicates that the action takes place over a short period of time. It's also used for a softer, more gentler tone. 我去看看你, I'll go and visit you. Later on, Huang Renhao says 咱们下去问问吧.

4. 还有别的办法吗?

Is there any other way?

5. 先拨上海的区号，接着拨电话号码。

First dial the area code for Shanghai, then dial the telephone number. 区号 literally means area number, an area code. 接着 means following. We could also use the same sentence pattern with 然后, as before. 先拨上海的区号，然后拨电话号码。

6. 占线。

It's busy.

文化背景（Sign Posts）

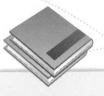

Making Calls in China

Making phone calls in China is much easier and cheaper than it used to be. At most hotels, you can dial directly from your room, although, as we saw in the dialogue, a deposit is often required. Sometimes you can simply have the front desk swipe your credit card as a deposit.

Local calls are usually 7 or 8 digits, depending on the city. Large cities like Beijing switched to 8 digit numbers several years ago. The largest cities have a two digit area code. "10" for Beijing, "21" for Shanghai. Smaller locations have 3 digit area codes. For example, Chengde to the north of Beijing is 314. To make a domestic long distance call, you usually dial 0, then the area code followed by the local number. For long distance calls, you can also buy phone cards that give you heavily discounted rates on long distance charges.

10 digit phone numbers are also very common in China, and they usually start in 13. These are for cell phones. The numbers are longer because most of these phones can be used while roaming anywhere in China.

Rather than have a separate area code, the area code is built into each cell phone number. Cell phones are extremely common in China. At least in the cities, it seems just about everybody has one, from high school students to retired people. Cell phones are not very expensive, so it makes sense to buy one if you are in China for more than just a few weeks. For shorter trips, you can even rent cell phones.

旅游汉语

语言点 (Bookmarks)

1. 正好 indicates a convenient coincidence

你要去邮局吗?正好帮我寄封信。

Are you going to the post office? What a coincidence! You can help me mail a letter.

今天我正好有时间,咱们一块去吧。

It's just so happened that I have time today. Let's go together.

2. 怎么 how

请问,去故宫怎么走?

May I ask how do you get to the Forbidden City?

你知道怎么去动物园比较快?

Do you know how to get to the zoo fairly quickly?

句型与替换练习
(Substitution & Extention)

1. 正……呢 indicates that something is ongoing

昨天下雨的时候，我们正爬长城呢。

We were right in the middle of climbing the Great Wall when it rained yesterday.

替换例句：

她正看电视呢。

他正等着我们呢。

2. 先……，然后…… first something, then something else

我们先去颐和园，然后再去爬长城。

Let's go to the Summer Palace first, and then we'll go to the Great Wall.

替换例句：

你们先买电话卡，然后才能在房间里打电话。

你们先交押金，然后才能拿到房间钥匙。

3. V+V indicates a short period of time, or brings a softer tone to the sentence

太累了，休息休息吧。

Too tired. Let's take a break.

替换例句：

出去之前我们先看看地图吧。

请尝尝这道菜好不好吃。

第 8 课

换钱
Change Money

¥

旅游汉语

课文 (Text)

Huáng Rénháo: Míngtiān zánmen qù nǎr chī fàn?
黄 人豪 : 明天 咱们 去哪儿吃饭?

Xuěméi: Nǐ shuō ne? Shì zài fàndiàn chī háishi chūqù chī?
雪梅: 你 说 呢? 是 在 饭店 吃 还是 出去 吃?

Huáng Rénháo: Háishi chūqù chī ba. Ài, zánmen chī shuàn yángròu
黄 人豪 : 还是 出去 吃 吧。哎, 咱们 吃 涮 羊肉

zěnmeyàng?
怎么样?

Xuěméi: Hǎo!
雪梅: 好!

Huáng Rénháo: Wǒ xiǎng háishi yīnggāi xiān yùdìng yīxiàr.
黄 人豪 : 我 想 还是 应该 先 预订 一下儿。

Xuěméi: Duì, wǒmen hái yīnggāi qù huàn qián.
雪梅: 对, 我们 还 应该 去 换 钱。

Huáng Rénháo: Zánmen yīqǐ qù ba.
黄 人豪 : 咱们 一起 去 吧。

Xuěméi: Èng, hǎo.
雪梅: 嗯, 好。

Yínháng rényuán: Nín hǎo, qǐng wèn bànlǐ shénme yèwù?
银行 人员 : 您 好, 请 问 办理 什么 业务?

Huáng Rénháo: Nín hǎo, wǒ xiǎng yòng Měiyuán huàn Rénmínbì.

黄 人豪： 您好，我想 用 美元 换 人民币。

Yínháng rényuán: Qǐng tián yīxiàr zhè zhāng dānzi.

银行 人员 ： 请 填 一下儿这 张 单子。

Huáng Rénháo: Jīntiān de huìlǜ shì duōshao?

黄 人豪 ： 今天的 汇率是 多少？

Yínháng rényuán: Měiyuán de màichūjià shì 8.26 .

银行 人员 ： 美元 的 卖出价是 8.26。

Huáng Rénháo: Ō, huàn 500 Měiyuán ba.

黄 人豪： 噢，换 500 美元 吧。

Yínháng rényuán: Qǐng gěi wǒ kànkan nín de hùzhào.

银行 人员 ： 请 给我 看看 您的 护照。

Huáng Rénháo: Hǎo.

黄 人豪： 好。

Yínháng rényuán: Qǐng zài zhè zhāng dānzi shàng qiānzì.

银行 人员 ： 请 在 这 张 单子 上 签字。

Huáng Rénháo: Hǎo de. Zài nǎr qiān ya?

黄 人豪： 好 的。在 哪儿 签 呀？

Yínháng rényuán: Yòuxiàjiǎo.

银行 人员 ： 右下角。

Xuěméi: Zhèlǐ.

雪梅：这里。

Yínháng rényuán: Zhè shì nín huàn de Rénmínbì, nín diǎn yīxiàr.
银行 人员 ： 这是 您 换 的 人民币，您 点 一下儿。

Huáng Rénháo: Méi wèntí, xièxie.
黄 人豪 ： 没 问题，谢谢。

Yínháng rényuán: Bù kèqi.
银行 人员 ： 不 客气。

Biǎojiě: Rénháo!
表姐： 人豪!

Huáng Rénháo: Biǎojiě! Kuài qǐng jìn.
黄 人豪 ： 表姐! 快 请进。

Xuěméi: Biǎojiě, nǐ hǎo ma?
雪梅： 表姐，你 好 吗?

Biǎojiě: Tǐng hǎo de.
表姐： 挺 好 的。

Xuěméi: Kuài qǐng zuò.
雪梅： 快 请 坐。

Biǎojiě: Xièxie. Rénháo, nǐmen liǎ dōu méi shénme biànhuà,
表姐： 谢谢。人豪，你们俩 都 没 什么 变化，

Xuěméi háishi nàme niánqīng.
雪梅 还是 那么 年轻。

Huáng Rénháo: Zhè shì Liú Yǒng ba? Dōu zhème gāo le.
黄 人豪 ： 这 是 刘 勇 吧? 都 这么 高 了。

Biǎojiě: Yǐjīng shì dàxué èrniánjí de xuésheng le.
表姐: 已经 是 大学 二年级 的 学生 了。

Xuěméi: Shíjiān guò de zhēn kuài, shàngcì wǒ lái de shíhou,
雪梅: 时间 过 得 真 快，上次 我 来 的 时候，

tā hái shì gè xiǎo háizi ne!
他 还 是 个 小 孩子 呢!

Biǎojiě: Nà shíhou tā hái shàng xiǎoxué ne.
表姐: 那 时候 他 还 上 小学 呢。

Liú Yǒng: Ài, Xiǎojié ne?
刘 勇: 哎，小杰 呢?

Huáng Rénháo: Xiǎojié qù mǎi jiāojuǎn le.
黄 人豪: 小杰 去 买 胶卷 了。

Liú Yǒng: Mài jiāojuǎn de hěn duō, fàndiàn pángbiānr jiù yǒu.
刘 勇: 卖 胶卷 的 很 多，饭店 旁边儿 就 有。

Huáng Rénháo: Tā yào mǎi hēibái jiāojuǎn, hǎoxiàng zhèlǐ bù hǎo mǎi ba.
黄 人豪: 她 要 买 黑白胶卷，好像 这里 不 好 买 吧。

Xuěméi: Zhè gè háizi hěn xǐhuan shèyǐng, tèbié shì hēibái de.
雪梅: 这 个 孩子 很 喜欢 摄影，特别 是 黑白 的。

Liú Yǒng: Xiànzài hēibái jiāojuǎn tài shǎo le.
刘 勇: 现在 黑白 胶卷 太 少 了。

Huáng Rénháo: Kěnéng Xiǎojié huílái le.
黄 人豪: 可能 小杰 回来 了。

Huang Renhao: Where should we eat tomorrow?

Xuemei: What do you think? Should we eat at the hotel or somewhere outside?

Huang Renhao: Let's eat somewhere out of the hotel. How about having lamb hotpot?

Xuemei: Great!

Huang Renhao: I think we should make a booking.

Xuemei: Yes, we should also change some money.

Huang Renhao: Let's go together.

Xuemei: Great!

Bank clerk: Hi! What can I do for you?

Huang Renhao: Hi! I'd like to change some RMB with US dollars.

Bank clerk: Please fill in this form.

Huang Renhao: What's the exchange rate today?

Bank clerk: The sell rate for US dollars is 8.26.

Huang Renhao: I'll change 500 dollars.

Bank clerk: Please show me your passport.

Huang Renhao: OK.

Bank clerk: Sign the form, please.

Huang Renhao: Where do I sign?

Bank clerk: At the bottom right hand corner.

Xuemei: Here.

Bank clerk: This is your RMB, please count it.

Huang Renhao: No problem. Thank you!

Bank clerk: You're welcome!

Cousin: Renhao!

Huang Renhao: Cousin! Come in please.

Xuemei: Cousin, how are you?

Cousin: Pretty good.

Xuemei: Take a seat!

Cousin: Thank you. You two haven't changed much, Xuemei still looks young as ever.

Huang Renhao: This must be Liu Yong?He's so tall already.

Cousin: He's already a second year university student.

Xuemei: Time passes so quickly, last time when I came he was still a kid!

Cousin: He was still in primary school then.

Liu Yong: Where's Xiaojie?

Huang Renhao: She's gone to buy films.

Liu Yong: You can buy films everywhere, even right next to the hotel.

Huang Renhao: She wants to buy black and white films, they're not so easy to buy here.

Xuemei: The girl really likes photography, especially in black and white.

Liu Yong: Black and white films are so rare these days.

Huang Renhao: Maybe Xiaojie's back.

旅游汉语

生词（New Words）

1. 涮羊肉	shuàn yángròu		lamb hotpot
2. 换钱	huànqián		exchange money
3. 银行	yínháng	名	bank
4. 业务	yèwù	名	business
5. 美元	Měiyuán	名	U.S. dollar
6. 人民币	Rénmínbì	名	RMB
7. 单子	dānzi	名	bill
8. 汇率	huìlǜ	名	exchange rate
9. 卖	mài	动	sell
10. 签字	qiānzì	动	sign
11. 那么	nàme	代	like that
12. 年轻	niánqīng	形	young
13. 好像	hǎoxiàng	副	as if
14. 孩子	háizi	名	child

15. 摄影	shèyǐng	名	photography
16. 特别	tèbié	副	particularly

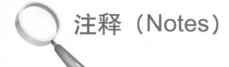

注释 (Notes)

1. 涮羊肉

涮羊肉 is a popular meal in Beijing, but usually you have this in a local restaurant outside the hotel. 涮 means to cook by dipping in boiling water or sauce of some kind, like a fondue. 羊肉 is mutton, or lamb. So 涮羊肉 is lamb hotpot, a Beijing specialty.

2. 应该先预订一下。

We should make a reservation. 应该 means should. Remember we learned 预订 in a previous lesson. It means to make a reservation.

3. 挺好的。

挺好的 means just fine. 挺 means the same thing as 很.

4. 雪梅还是那么年轻。

Xuemei is still so young. 刘勇这么高了! Liu Yong is so tall now! 那么 and 这么 are both used to emphasize that something is different from what you expected. These are common things to say when people meet again after a long time apart.

文化背景（Sign Posts）

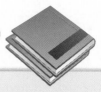

Changing Money

Renminbi, the Chinese currency, is not yet fully convertible. That means you can't just take Renminbi and exchange (兑换) for foreign currency without a permit or other documentation. But it's easy to change from foreign currency into Renminbi.

The exchange rate is strictly regulated by the national government in China. No matter where you change money, at the airport, your hotel, a bank or even in major shopping areas, the rate is exactly the same. There should be no other fees or commissions charged.

If you have Chinese currency left over at the end of your trip, you can change this back into foreign currency provided that you have your original receipts from when you changed money the first time. Most people do this at the airport on their way out, as you may have to show your outbound plane ticket to prove you are leaving the country.

旅游汉语

语言点（Bookmarks）

1. 应该 should

去他家之前应该先给他打个电话。

Before we go to his house, we should give him a phone call.

今天天气很冷，你应该多穿点儿衣服。

Today is really cold. You should wear more clothing.

2. 那么/这么 both indicate more than expected

没想到北京的夏天这么热。

I never expected the summer in Beijing was so hot.

没想到上海的汽车那么多。

I never knew that there were so many cars in Shanghai.

3. 挺 a fair amount

学汉语挺有意思的。

It's kind of interesting to learn Chinese.

去爬长城挺累的。

It's somewhat tiring to climb the Great Wall.

句型与替换练习
（Substitution & Extention）

1. (是)……还是…… indicating a choice

你喝茶还是喝咖啡?

Would you drink tea or would you drink coffee?

你是想去北京还是想去上海?

Would you like to go to Beijing or would you like to go to Shanghai?

替换例句:

> 你喜欢打篮球还是喜欢踢足球?
>
> 我们是坐飞机去呢，还是坐火车去呢?

2. (不)好+ V indicates the verb is easy or not easy to do

这首歌很好唱。

This song is really easy to sing.

这个字不太好写。

This character is not very easy to write.

替换例句:

> 这家饭店就在路边，很好找。
>
> 现在的火车票不太好买。

第9课

发传真
Send A Fax

旅游汉语

课文 (Text)

Huáng Rénháo: Nín hǎo!
黄 人豪 ：您 好！

Fúwùyuán: Nín hǎo!
服务员：您 好！

Huáng Rénháo: Wǒ xiǎng bǎ zhè fèn cáiliào hé zhè gè hùzhào fùyìn yīxiàr.
黄 人豪 ：我 想 把 这份 材料 和 这个 护照 复印 一下儿。

Fúwùyuán: Zhè fèn cáiliào shì dānmiàn yìn háishi shuāngmiàn yìn?
服务员：这份 材料 是 单面 印还是 双面 印？

Huáng Rénháo: Shuāngmiàn de ba.
黄 人豪 ： 双面 的吧。

Fúwùyuán: Hùzhào yìn nǎ yè?
服务员：护照 印哪页？

Huáng Rénháo: Dì-yī yè hé yǒu qiānzhèng de nà yī yè.
黄 人豪 ：第一 页和 有 签证 的那一 页。

Fúwùyuán: Fùyìn hǎo le, xiānsheng nín kànkan.
服务员：复印 好了，先生 您 看看。

Huáng Rénháo: Qiānzhèng shàngmiàn de xiàngpiàn yìn de bù tài qīngchu.
黄 人豪 ： 签证 上面 的 相片 印 得不太 清楚。

Fúwùyuán: Kěnéng fùyìnjī yǒudiǎnr wèntí. Duìbuqǐ, wǒ zài bāng
服务员： 可能 复印机 有点儿 问题。对不起，我 再 帮

nín chóng yìn yī zhāng.
您 重 印 一 张。

Fúwùyuán: Zhè gè zěnmeyàng?
服务员： 这个 怎么样？

Huáng Rénháo: Zhè gè fùyìn de búcuò.
黄 人豪： 这 个 复印 得 不错。

Huáng Rénháo: Nǐmen zhèr néng fā chuánzhēn ba, wǒ yào fā yī fēng
黄 人豪： 你们 这儿 能 发 传真 吧，我 要 发 一 封

chuánzhēn.
传真。

Fúwùyuán: Chuánzhēnjī zài zhèbian ne, nín zhèbian qǐng.
服务员： 传真机 在 这边 呢，您 这边 请。

Huáng Rénháo: Hǎo!
黄 人豪： 好！

Fúwùyuán: Guónèi de háishi guójì de?
服务员： 国内的还是 国际的？

Huáng Rénháo: Guójì de.
黄 人豪： 国际 的。

Fúwùyuán: Chuánzhēnhào shì duōshao?

服务员： 传真号 是 多少?

Huáng Rénhào: Gěi nǐ zhè zhāng zhǐ, shàngmiàn xiězhe chuánzhēnhào.

黄 人豪： 给你这 张 纸，上面 写着 传真号。

Fúwùyuán: Chuánzhēn fā hǎo le.

服务员： 传真 发好了。

Huáng Rénhào: Hǎo, xièxie! Duōshao qián?

黄 人豪： 好，谢谢! 多少 钱?

Fúwùyuán: Yīgòng 10 yuán qián.

服务员：一共 10 元 钱。

Huáng Rénhào: Hǎo, xièxie!

黄 人豪： 好，谢谢!

Xuěméi: Ài, lǎogōng, nǐ zài zhèr.

雪梅：哎，老公，你 在 这儿。

Huáng Rénhào: Xuěméi, wǒ lái fā chuánzhēn, nǐ ne?

黄 人豪： 雪梅，我来发 传真，你呢?

Xuěméi: Wǒ yào qù jì xìn, nǐ péi wǒ qù ba.

雪梅：我要 去寄信，你陪我去吧。

Huáng Rénhào: Hǎo! zǒu!

黄 人豪： 好! 走!

Huáng Rénháo: Shì jì gěi māma de ma?
黄 人豪：是寄给妈妈的吗？

Xuěméi: Shì de, suǒyǐ yào jì "airmail".
雪梅：是的，所以要寄"airmail"。

Huáng Rénháo: Nà jiù yào jì hángkōngxìn. Zhème zhòng a, zhè fēng
黄 人豪：那就要寄 航空信。这么 重 啊，这封

xìn kěndìng chāozhòng le.
信 肯定 超重 了。

Xuěméi: Yǒu shíjǐ zhāng zhàopiàn ne, quán shì Xiǎojié zhào de.
雪梅：有十几张 照片 呢，全是小杰照的。

Huáng Rénháo: Nà jiù jì guàhàoxìn ba, bié diū le.
黄 人豪：那就寄挂号信吧，别丢了。

Xuěméi: Guàhàoxìn shāowēi màn yīdiǎnr, děi shí tiān zuǒyòu.
雪梅：挂号信 稍微 慢 一点儿，得十天 左右。

Huáng Rénháo: Ài, kěshì ānquán a, zǒu ba, wǒ zhènghǎo yào mǎi
黄 人豪：唉，可是安全 啊，走吧，我 正好 要买

tào míngxìnpiàn ne.
套 明信片 呢。

Xuě méi: À, lǎogōng, yóujú zài zhèbian.
雪梅：啊，老公，邮局在 这边。

Huang Renhao: Hello!

Staff: Hello!

Huang Renhao: I'd like to photocopy this document and my passport.

Staff: Do I copy the document on one side or both sides?

Huang Renhao: Both sides, please.

Staff: Which pages of the passport shall I photocopy?

Huang Renhao: The first page and the one with a visa on it.

Staff: It's done, please have a look.

Huang Renhao: The photograph on the visa's not that clear.

Staff: Maybe our photocopier's having problems. Sorry, we'll redo one for you.

Staff: How's this?

Huang Renhao: That's a good copy.

Huang Renhao: You can send faxes here right? I'd like to send a fax.

Staff: The fax machine is here, please come over this side.

Huang Renhao: OK!

Staff: Domestic or international?

Huang Renhao: International.

Staff: What's the fax number?

Huang Renhao: Here, the fax number is written on this piece of paper.

Staff: The fax has gone through.

Huang Renhao: Great, thanks! How much is it?

Staff: 10 *yuan*.

Huang Renhao: OK, thank you!

Xuemei: Honey, here you are.

Huang Renhao: Xuemei, I came to send a fax, how about you?

Xuemei: I need to post a letter, why don't you come with me?

Huang Renhao: OK, let's go!

Huang Renhao: Is the letter for mom?

Xuemei: Yes, that's why it has to go by airmail.

Huang Renhao: Airmail it is. It's so heavy, this letter's over the weight limit for sure.

Xuemei: There are about a dozen photos, all taken by Xiaojie.

Huang Renhao: Then send it by registered mail, in case it gets lost.

Xuemei: Registered mail takes a little longer, about ten days.

Huang Renhao: Yeah, but it's safe. Come on, I have to buy some postcards anyway.

Xuemei: Uh, honey, the post office is this way.

旅游汉语

生词（New Words）

1. 材料	cáiliào	名	document
2. 复印	fùyìn	动	photocopy
3. 页	yè	量	page
4. 签证	qiānzhèng	名	visa
5. 相片	xiàngpiàn	名	photo
6. 重	chóng	副	again
7. 传真	chuánzhēn	名	fax
8. 老公	lǎogōng	名	husband
9. 陪	péi	动	accompany
10. 寄	jì	动	post
11. 所以	suǒyǐ	连	so
12. 航空信	hángkōngxìn	名	airmail
13. 肯定	kěndìng	形	sure
14. 超重	chāozhòng	形	overweight
15. 挂号信	guàhàoxìn	名	registered letter

16. 可是	kěshì	连	but
17. 安全	ānquán	形	safe
18. 明信片	míngxìnpiàn	名	postcard
19. 邮局	yóujú	名	post office

旅游汉语

注释（Notes）

1. 签证上的相片印得不太清楚。

得 is used to indicate the extent of a verb or adjective. In this case, 印得不太清楚, it's not printed very clearly.

2. 我再给帮重印一张。

We'll make another copy for you. 重 is to repeat. 重印 means to copy again.

3. 挂号信稍微慢一点儿，得十天左右吧。

Registered mail is a little slower, approximately ten days. 稍微 indicates just a slight amount, in this case perhaps a day or two. We just talked about this character 得 a moment ago. Here it serves a different purpose, and is pronounced differently: děi.

语言点（Bookmarks）

1. 得 to show the extent of an action

他汉语说得很好。

He speaks Chinese very well.

雨下得很大。

It's raining very heavily.

2. 稍微 a slight amount

他比你稍微高一点儿。

He is a little bit taller than you.

这个菜稍微有点儿咸.

This dish is a little salty.

3. 套 a set of something

我想买一套中国的邮票。

I'd like to buy a set of Chinese stamps.

你买的这套衣服很好看。

This set of clothing you bought is really attractive.

句型与替换练习
(Substitution & Extention)

1. V+好 indicating the action has been completed

去上海的机票已经买好了。

The air ticket for Shanghai has been bought.

替换例句：

请把这件行李放好。

您要的出租车已经订好了。

2. V+着 shows the action or state is continuing

她穿着红色的毛衣。

She is wearing a red sweater.

替换例句：

桌上放着一本儿字典。

门锁着呢，我进不去。

理发
Cut Hair

旅游汉语

课文（Text）

Fúwùyuán: Nín hǎo! Huānyíng guānglín!
服务员：您 好！欢迎　光临！

Fúwùyuán: Qǐng wèn zuò tóufa zuò měiróng?
服务员：请 问 做 头发 做 美容？

Xuěméi: Jiǎn tóufa.
雪梅：剪 头发。

Fúwùyuán: Xiān xǐ yī xǐ ba!
服务员：先 洗 一 洗 吧！

Xuěméi: Xíng, zěnme xǐ?
雪梅：行，怎么 洗？

Fúwùyuán: Wǒmen zhèr yǒu gānxǐ yě yǒu shīxǐ.
服务员：我们 这儿 有 干洗 也 有 湿洗。

Xuěméi: Gānxǐ xūyào duō cháng shíjiān?
雪梅：干洗 需要 多 长 时间？

Fúwùyuán: Jiāshàng tóubù ànmó bàn xiǎoshí.
服务员：加上 头部 按摩 半 小时。

Xuěméi: Hǎo, gānxǐ ba, zhènghǎo wǒ yǒudiǎnr lèi le.
雪梅：好，干洗 吧，正好　我 有点儿 累 了。

Fúwùyuán: Dào zhèbianr chōng yīxiàr shuǐ ba.
服务员：到 这边儿 冲 一下儿 水 吧。

Xuěméi: Xièxie!
雪梅：谢谢!

Xuěméi: Shuǐ yǒuyīdiǎnr rè.
雪梅：水 有一点儿 热。

Fúwùyuán: Duìbuqǐ, wǒ tiáo yīxiàr. Xiànzài kěyǐ le ma?
服务员：对不起，我 调 一下儿。现在 可以 了 吗?

Xuěméi: Kěyǐ le.
雪梅：可以 了。

Fúwùyuán: Xǐ hǎo le, nín dào nàbian shāo děng yīxià, lǐfàshī
服务员：洗 好 了，您 到 那边 稍 等 一下，理发师

gěi nín lǐfà.
给 您 理发。

Xuěméi: Hǎode, xièxie nín.
雪梅：好的，谢谢 您。

Lǐfàshī: Nín hǎo, nín xiǎng zěnme jiǎn?
理发师：您 好，您 想 怎么 剪?

Xuěméi: Fàxíng bù biàn, jiǎn duǎn yīdiǎnr.
雪梅：发型 不 变，剪 短 一点儿。

Lǐfàshī: Qiánbian jiǎn qí le ma?
理发师：前边 剪 齐 了 吗?

Xuěméi: Duì! Liǎngbiānr jiǎn báo yīdiǎnr.

雪梅： 对！ 两边儿 剪 薄 一点儿。

Lǐfàshī : Nín kàn qù duōshao héshì?

理发师： 您 看 去 多少 合适？

Xuěméi: "Qù" duōshao? Qù nǎli?

雪梅： "去" 多少？ 去 哪里？

Lǐfàshī : Ō! Jiùshì "jiǎn diào" duōshao?

理发师： 噢！就是 "剪掉" 多少？

Xuěméi: Jiǎn diào yī límǐ, bù shì bù shì, "qù" yī límǐ.

雪梅： 剪 掉 一 厘米，不 是 不 是，"去" 一 厘米。

Lǐfàshī : Èng, hǎo de.

理发师： 嗯， 好 的。

Lǐfàshī : Zhè gè fàxíng hěn shìhé nín.

理发师： 这个 发型 很 适合 您。

Xuěméi: Xièxie!

雪梅： 谢谢！

Lǐfàshī : Rúguǒ shāowēi tàng yīxiàr kěnéng huì gèng hǎo yīxiē,

理发师： 如果 稍微 烫 一下儿 可能 会 更 好 一些，

nín xiǎng shìshi ma?

您 想 试试 吗？

Xuěméi: Bù yòng, wǒ bù xǐhuan tàng tóufa.

雪梅： 不用，我 不 喜欢 烫 头发。

Lǐfàshī:　Jiǎn hǎo le,　nín kàn xíng ma?
理发师： 剪 好 了，您 看 行 吗？

Xuěméi:　Èng, hòubian kěyǐ zài duǎn yīdiǎnr ma?
雪梅： 嗯，后边 可以 再 短 一点儿 吗？

Lǐfàshī:　Nín kàn zhèyàng xíng ma?
理发师： 您 看 这样 行 吗？

Xuěméi:　Jiù zhèyàng ba!
雪梅： 就 这样 吧！

Lǐfàshī:　Chuīfēng ma?
理发师： 吹风 吗？

Xuěméi:　Chuīfēng.
雪梅： 吹风。

Xuěméi:　Qǐng wèn zài nǎr jiāo qián ne?
雪梅： 请 问 在 哪儿 交 钱 呢？

Fúwùyuán:　Zài nàbiān guìtái shàng, wǒ dài nín qù.
服务员： 在 那边 柜台 上，我 带 您 去。

Xuěméi:　Xièxie! Wǒ zìjǐ qù ba!
雪梅： 谢谢！我 自己 去 吧！

Fúwùyuán:　Hǎo de.
服务员： 好 的。

Staff: Hello! Welcome!

Staff: Are you having your hair done or a beauty treatment?

Xuemei: A haircut.

Staff: We'll give it a wash first!

Xuemei: Sure, what sort of wash?

Staff: We have dry and wet washes here.

Xuemei: How long is the dry wash?

Staff: It's half an hour including the head massage.

Xuemei: OK, I'll have a dry wash, just as well I'm a little tired.

Staff: Come over here and we'll give it a rinse.

Xuemei: Thanks!

Xuemei: The water is a little hot.

Staff: Sorry, I'll adjust it. Is it alright now?

Xuemei: It's fine.

Staff: It's ready. Can you wait over there, a hairdresser will be with you shortly.

Xuemei: Ok, thank you.

Hairdresser: Hello, what sort of haircut would you like?

Xuemei: Keep the style, just cut it a bit shorter.

Hairdresser: Keep the front even?

Xuemei: That's right! Thin the two sides a little.

Hairdresser: How much do you want off?

Xuemei: How much do I want off? Where?

Hairdresser: Oh! As in "cut off"?

Xuemei: Cut off one centimetre, no no, take "off" one centimetre.

Hairdresser: OK.

Hairdresser: This hairstyle really suits you.

Xuemei: Thank you!

Hairdresser: If you give it a slight perm it might look even better, would you like to try it?

Xuemei: No, I don't like perms.

Hairdresser: It's ready, do you think it's OK?

Xuemei: Can you make it a bit shorter at the back?

Hairdresser: Sure, how does this look?

Xuemei: That'll do!

Hairdresser: Would you like your hair blowdried?

Xuemei: Yes, please.

Xuemei: Where do I pay?

Staff: At the counter over there, I'll take you there.

Xuemei: Thanks! I'll go there myself!

Staff: Sure.

旅游汉语

生词（New Words）

1. 欢迎	huānyíng	动	welcome
2. 光临	guānglín	动	presence of a guest
3. 头发	tóufa	名	hair
4. 美容	měiróng	名	have a facial
5. 剪	jiǎn	动	cut
6. 冲	chōng	动	rinse
7. 调	tiáo	动	adjust
8. 理发	lǐfà	动	have a haircut
9. 发型	fàxíng	名	hair style
10. 一点儿	yīdiǎnr	量	a bit
11. 薄	báo	形	thin
12. 合适	héshì	形	suitable
13. 厘米	límǐ	名	centimeter
14. 适合	shìhé	动	suit
15. 如果	rúguǒ	连	if

16. 稍微	shāowēi	副	a little
17. 烫	tàng	动	perm
18. 吹风	chuīfēng	动	dry hair

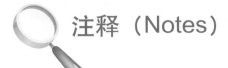

旅游汉语

🔍 注释（Notes）

1. 您今天是做头发还是做美容。

Are you having your hair done or a makeover today?

2. 我们这儿有干洗也有湿洗。

We have a dry wash and a wet wash. 也 is used to show two equal options.

3. 水有一点儿热。

The water is a little hot. 有一点儿 is like the expression 稍微 we learned earlier, to indicate a small extent.

4. 发型不变，剪短一点儿。

Don't change the style, just cut it a little shorter. 剪短 is to cut short. 剪齐 is to cut even. 前边剪齐 is to cut the bangs evenly. 剪薄 is to thin the hair out. 两边儿剪薄点儿 is to thin the sides out a little.

5. 去多少？

Where is the hair going? Here, 去 simply means to cut off（剪掉）. 去多少 just means 剪掉多少.

语言点 （Bookmarks）

1. 也 also

她会说英语，也会说日语。

She speaks English and she can also speak Japanese.

我去过上海，也去过北京。

I've been to Shanghai and I've been to Beijing.

2. 适合 suitable for something

绿茶适合夏天喝。

Green tea is more suitable for drinking in the summer.

这件衣服的颜色不适合你。

The colour of this clothing is not suitable for you.

3. 更 even more

下了一夜雨，天气更冷了。

It rains all night. The weather is even colder now.

他比我更了解中国文化。

He knows a lot more about Chinese culture than I do.

句型与替换练习
(Substitution & Extention)

1. 有 (一) 点儿 a little, slightly

　　这个饭店离市中心有点儿远。

　　This hotel is a little far from the downtown area.

　　我今天有一点儿不舒服。

　　Today I'm a little bit uncomfortable.

　　替换例句：

　　　　这件衣服有点儿大。

　　　　这个菜有一点儿咸。

第11课

洗衣服务
Laundry Service

旅游汉语

课文（Text）

Xuě méi: Qǐng shāo děng.
雪梅：请 稍 等。

Fúwùyuán: Nǐ hǎo!
服务员：你好!

Xuěméi: Nǐ hǎo!
雪梅：你好!

Fúwùyuán: Wǒ shì kèfángbù de, wǒ lái qǔ yīfu.
服务员：我 是 客房部 的，我 来 取 衣服。

Xuěméi: Qǐng jìn. Yīfu zài zhèr.
雪梅：请 进。衣服 在 这儿。

Fúwùyuán: Wǒ xiān kànkan. Fūrén, zhè jiàn chènshān shǎo le yī
服务员：我 先 看看。夫人，这件 衬衫 少 了 一

gè kòuzi.
个 扣子。

Xuěméi: Èng, wǒ zhīdao.
雪梅：嗯，我 知道。

Fúwùyuán: Xǐ zhèxiē yīfu yǒu shénme yāoqiú ma?
服务员：洗 这些 衣服 有 什么 要求 吗?

雪梅： 这 几 件 衣服 要 干洗。这 件 缩水，千万

不 要 水洗。

雪梅： 这 件 衬衫 的 袖子 上 有 块 污渍，能

洗掉 吗？

服务员： 我 看看 这是 什么 东西。好像 是 酱油。

雪梅： 可能 是 酱油。

服务员： 我们 只 能 尽量 洗。

雪梅： 不 能 洗掉 吗？

服务员： 能 不 能 洗掉 没有 把握。

服务员： 这些 衣服 都 要 熨 吧！

旅游汉语

Xuěméi: Dāngrán, xǐ wán yào yùn hǎo.

雪梅： 当然，洗完要熨好。

Fúwùyuán: Hǎo de, wǒ jì xiàlái le.

服务员： 好的，我记下来了。

Xuěméi: Duō cháng shíjiān néng xǐwán ne?

雪梅： 多 长 时间 能 洗完 呢？

Fúwùyuán: Míngtiān xiàwǔ jiù kěyǐ gěi nín sòng huílái.

服务员： 明天 下午 就 可以 给您 送 回来。

Xuěméi: Zěnme fùfèi?

雪梅： 怎么 付费？

Fúwùyuán: Nín jiézhàng tuìfáng de shíhou kěyǐ yīqǐ fù.

服务员： 您 结账 退房 的 时候 可以 一起 付。

Xuěméi: Hǎo de!

雪梅： 好 的!

Fúwùyuán: Nín zài quèrèn yīxiàr yīfu de jiànshù hé xǐyī yāoqiú.

服务员：您 再 确认 一下儿 衣服 的 件数 和 洗衣 要求。

Xuěméi: Méi wèntí.

雪梅： 没 问题。

Fúwùyuán: Méi wèntí de huà, qǐng nín qiān gè zì.

服务员：没 问题 的 话，请 您 签 个 字。

Xuěméi: Xièxie!

雪梅：谢谢！

Fúwùyuán: Bùkèqi!

服务员：不客气！

Xuěméi: Ō, duìbuqǐ, qǐng ràng wǒ kànkan háizi de yīfu lǐmiàn

雪梅：噢，对不起，请 让 我 看看 孩子的 衣服 里面

yǒu méiyǒu dōngxi?

有 没有 东西？

Fúwùyuán: Nín shì shuō zhè jiàn ba?

服务员：您是 说 这件吧？

Xuěméi: Duì, wǒ kànkan kǒudai lǐ. Ài, hái zhēn yǒu dōngxi.

雪梅：对，我 看看 口袋 里。哎，还 真 有 东西。

Xuěméi: Xièxie!

雪梅：谢谢！

Fúwùyuán: Bù kèqi!

服务员：不 客气！

Xuemei: Just a minute.

Staff: Hello!

Xuemei: Hello!

Staff: I'm from housekeeping, I've come to collect the laundry.

Xuemei: Please come in. The clothes are here.

Staff: Let me see. Madam, this shirt is missing a button.

Xuemei: I know.

Staff: Do you have any requirements for laundering these garments?

Xuemei: These garments need to be drycleaned. This one is easy to shrink, please don't wash it in water.

Xuemei: This shirt has a stain on the sleeve, can it be washed off?

Staff: Let's see, what is this? It looks like soy sauce.

Xuemei: It may be soy sauce.

Staff: We can try our best.

Xuemei: You can't get it off?

Staff: We're not sure whether it can be washed off.

Staff: I take it these garments all need to be pressed!

Xuemei: Of course, they need to be pressed after they're cleaned.

Staff: Sure, I've taken that down.

Xuemei: How long does it take?

Staff: We can bring it back tomorrow afternoon.

Xuemei: How do I pay?

Staff: You can pay when you check out as part of your room bill.

Xuemei: Great!

Staff: Please confirm the number of garments and your laundry requirements.

Xuemei: No problem.

Staff: If it's all OK, please sign here.

Xuemei: Thank you!

Staff: You're welcome!

Xuemei: Sorry, just let me see if there's anything in my daughter's clothes?

Staff: This must be the one you're talking about?

Xuemei: Yes, let me check the pockets. There really is something.

Xuemei: Thanks!

Staff: You're welcome!

旅游汉语

生词（New Words）

1. 取	qǔ	动	take
2. 夫人	fūrén	名	Madam
3. 衬衫	chènshān	名	shirt
4. 扣子	kòuzi	名	button
5. 要求	yāoqiú	名	requirement
6. 缩水	suōshuǐ	动	shrink (of cloth)
7. 千万	qiānwàn	副	by all means
8. 袖子	xiùzi	名	sleeve
9. 污渍	wūzì	名	stain
10. 酱油	jiàngyóu	名	soy sauce
11. 尽量	jìnliàng	副	as much as possible
12. 把握	bǎwò	名	confidence
13. 熨	yùn	动	iron
14. 确认	quèrèn	动	confirm
15. 口袋	kǒudai	名	pocket

注释（Notes）

1. 这件衬衫少了一个扣子。
   This shirt is missing a button.

2. 这件缩水，千万不要水洗。
   Dry-cleaning 干洗 or regular wash with water 水洗.
   This piece shrinks in water, it absolutely must not be washed in water.

3. 我们只能尽量洗。
   We can only try our best to wash it. 尽量 is to the best of our ability.

4. 能不能洗掉没有把握。
   I'm not confident that we can wash it out. 把握 is confidence, it literally means grasp, like having a good grasp of the situation. 洗掉 is to wash away.

5. 您再确认一下儿衣服的件数和洗衣要求。
   Please check again the number of articles and washing instructions.

6. 还真有东西。
   There really is something.

旅游汉语

语言点 (Bookmarks)

1. 只能 the only choice

我的钱不够，只能买最便宜的票。

I don't have enough money. I can only buy the cheapest ticket.

今天下雨，我们只能一直呆在饭店里不能出去。

It's raining today, we have to stay in the hotel.

今天的时间不多了，我们只能去一个地方旅游。

We don't have much time today. We can only go to one place.

2. 尽量 as much as possible

明天的会很重要，请大家尽量参加。

Tomorrow's meeting is really important. Everyone makes sure that you can attend.

出去旅行要尽量少带点行李。

When we go out traveling, we should take as little luggage as possible.

我会尽量早点回来。

I'll come back as soon as I can.

3. 把握 confidence, sureness

能不能爬到山顶，我没有把握。

I'm not sure that I'll be able to climb to the top of the mountain.

我们没有把握订到明天的火车票。

We are not sure that we would be able to reserve the train tickets for tomorrow.

能不能找到您要的那张画，我们没有把握。

We are not sure that we'll be able to find the painting that you are looking for.

句型与替换练习
(Substitution & Extention)

1. V+回来 the result of action

她昨天买回来很多好吃的东西。

Yesterday she brought a lot of tasty things back.

替换例句：

他给我带回来一套明信片。

我没坐车，是走回来的。

投诉
Complaint

旅游汉语

课文（Text）

Jīnglǐ: Nín hǎo! Wǒ shì kèfángbù jīnglǐ, tīngshuō nín xǐ de
经理：您 好!我 是 客房部 经理，听说 您 洗 的

yīfu yǒu wèntí.
衣服 有 问题。

Xuěméi: Shì de, wǒ de zhè jiàn chènshān méiyǒu xǐ gānjìng.
雪梅：是 的，我 的 这件 衬衫 没有 洗 干净。

Jīnglǐ: Ō, zhè jiù shì nà kuài jiàngyóu wūzì. Wǒmen kěyǐ bǎ
经理：噢，这 就 是 那块 酱油 污渍。我们 可以 把

chènshān zài xǐ yī biàn.
衬衫 再 洗 一 遍。

Xuěméi: OK, Xièxie.
雪梅：OK，谢谢。

Jīnglǐ: Hěn bàoqiàn, wǒmen kěyǐ miǎn shōu nín de xǐyī fèiyòng.
经理：很 抱歉，我们 可以 免 收 您 的 洗衣 费用。

Xuěméi: Hǎo de, xièxie.
雪梅：好 的，谢谢。

Jīnglǐ: Bù kèqi, zàijiàn.
经理：不 客气，再见。

Xuěméi: Láojià, wǒ hái yǒu yī gè wèntí.
雪梅：劳驾，我还有一个问题。

Jīnglǐ: Nín qǐng jiǎng.
经理：您请讲。

Xuěméi: Wǒmen fángjiān de chōushuǐmǎtǒng lòushuǐ, érqiě yuè
雪梅：我们房间的抽水马桶漏水，而且越

lái yuè lìhai.
来越厉害。

Jīnglǐ: Zhēn duìbuqǐ.
经理：真对不起。

Xuěméi: Yǐjīng liǎng tiān le, shuìjiào de shíhou hěn chǎo, érqiě
雪梅：已经两天了，睡觉的时候很吵，而且

yě làngfèi shuǐ a.
也浪费水啊。

Jīnglǐ: Nín shuō de duì, wǒmen mǎshàng pài rén qù xiū.
经理：您说得对，我们马上派人去修。

Xuěméi: Hǎo de.
雪梅：好的。

Hello! I'm the housekeeping manager.

Manager: Hello! I'm the housekeeping manager. I heard that there is a problem with your laundry.

Xuemei: Yes, my shirt wasn't washed properly.

Manager: Oh, this is the soy sauce stain. We can wash that shirt again.

Xuemei: OK, Thank you.

Manager: Sorry about that. We can waive your laundry charges.

Xuemei: Great, thank you.

Manager: You're welcome, see you later.

Xuemei: Sorry, I have another problem.

Manager: Go ahead.

Xuemei: The toilet in our room leaks and it's getting worse.

Manager: I'm really sorry about that.

Xuemei: It's already been two days. It's very noisy when we try to sleep at night. Besides it's a waste of water.

Manager: You're right. We'll send someone to fix it right away.

Xuemei: OK.

生词 （New Words）

1. 经理	jīnglǐ	名	manager
2. 听说	tīngshuō	动	hear of
3. 干净	gānjìng	形	clean
4. 遍	biàn	量	(for action) once through
5. 免	miǎn	动	exempt
6. 费用	fèiyòng	名	expense
7. 劳驾	láojià	动	excuse me
8. 抽水马桶	chōushuǐ mǎtǒng	名	flush toilet
9. 漏	lòu	动	leak
10. 而且	érqiě	连	and also
11. 越来越	yuè lái yuè		more and more
12. 厉害	lìhai	形	terrible
13. 吵	chǎo	形	noisy
14. 浪费	làngfèi	动	waste
15. 修	xiū	动	repair

注释 （Notes）

1. 衬衫没有洗干净。

The shirt was not cleaned. It may have been washed (洗),
but it was not cleaned (洗干净), the stain is still there. The
manager knows just what she's talking about.

2. 那块酱油污渍

That soy sauce stain. 污 is something dirty. 污渍 is a
stain.

3. 我们可以把衬衫再洗一遍。

We can wash the shirt again. 再 indicates "again"，再洗
一遍, wash it again. For example, we could say 再读一遍,
read it again. 再说一遍, say it one more time. We learned
this sentence structure using 把 in a previous lesson. This is
a way to put the object before the verb, to put more emphasis
on the object. 把衣服洗干净, to clean the clothing.

4. 我们可以免收您的洗衣费用。

we can cancel the laundry charge this time. 免 means to
avoid or to do without. 免收, to not collect. 免费 means
no charge, for free, this is like a short form of 免收费用,
simply 免费. Here's an related vocabulary item 免洗, to not
require washing.

5. 劳驾

劳驾 is a good, polite way to attract someone's attention, or to ask for help.

6. 越来越厉害了。

It's getting worse. 越来越 is a very useful pattern for describing something that is getting more and more of some way. 越来越好, better and better. In this case, it's 越来越厉害, worse and worse, or more and more severe. We're going to learn more about this pattern later on. 厉害 means severe, to a severe extent, like 他病得很厉害, he's gravely ill, he's very sick.

7. 夜里睡觉的时候很吵，而且也浪费水呀。

而且 is another way of saying furthermore or in addition. It's very noisy at night when we're sleeping, furthermore, it wastes water. Here, the character 费 is used as a verb. It doesn't mean the same thing as 费用, which we learned above. As a verb, 费 means to waste, or to expend.

8. 我们马上派人去修。

We'll send someone to fix it right away. 派 is to send or to designate.

文化背景（Sign Posts）

Hotels in China (2)

There is a wide range of hotel accommodation in China, and a correspondingly wide range of services offered in hotels. The low end of the scale can be very basic and it's usually difficult to find any English service or western amenities at all. For example, many low-end hotels in China may not even serve coffee with breakfast, as, of course, most Chinese prefer tea. But when we look at the opposite end of the spectrum, the 5-star hotels in major cities like Beijing, Shanghai, and Guangzhou, the sky is the limit in terms of service and cost. In my personal experience, service at 5-star hotels in China actually exceeds what you would normally find in the West.

Hotels in China are rated on a 5-star system. Many low-end hotels are not even rated, so even a one or two star hotel has to maintain a certain level of service. These standards are enforced by the tourism authorities in China. Many 4 and 5 star hotels are run by international hotel chains and maintain a level of service that you would expect to find anywhere in the world. Most of these would include satellite television, laundry and dry cleaning, foreign currency exchange, and restaurants serving western as well as Chinese food. Many will even accept foreign credit cards and have extra services like a fitness centre with gym equipment and a swimming pool. Internet access is becoming more common in Chinese hotels, either at a centralized business centre or directly from the room through a high-speed connection. When dealing with 5 star hotels, you can increasingly assume they will have all these services. The very top end hotels are also increasingly offering services like child care and facilities for people with disabilities. Of course, as is the case anywhere, services and products offered for sale inside the hotel will often be more expensive than similar products and services sold outside. You pay for the convenience.

 语言点（Bookmarks）

1. 而且 furthermore

这里离市中心比较远，而且交通也不方便。

It's relatively far to the city center from here, and the transportation is no convenient.

他会开车，而且还会自己修车。

Not only can he drive a car, he also knows how to repair cars.

她会跳舞，而且歌也唱得不错。

She can dance, and she also sings pretty well.

2. 派 to send or designate sb.

他是公司派来的。

He was sent by the company.

我们会很快派人来和您联系。

We'll send someone very quickly to contact you.

别着急，我们会派专家去把电脑修好的。

Don't worry. We'll send an expert to fix the computer.

句型与替换练习
（Substitution & Extention）

1. 越来越 more and more

他会说的句子越来越多。

He can say more and more.

这种样式的衣服越来越受欢迎。

The style of clothing is increasingly popular.

替换例句：

天气越来越冷了。

他做的菜越来越好吃了。

第13课

运动健身
Do Exercise

课文 (Text)

Fúwùyuán: Huānyíng guānglín! Nín hǎo!
服务员： 欢迎　光临! 您 好!

Xiǎojié: Wǒmen kěyǐ shǐyòng zhè zhāng kǎ ma?
小杰： 我们 可以 使用 这 张 卡 吗?

Fúwùyuán: Kěyǐ, zhè shì jìcìkǎ.
服务员：可以，这 是 记次卡。

Liú Yǒng: Zhè zhāng kǎ kěyǐ shǐyòng duōshao cì?
刘 勇： 这 张 卡 可以 使用 多少 次?

Fúwùyuán: Zhè zhāng kǎ shì 30 cì de.
服务员： 这 张 卡 是 30 次 的。

Liú Yǒng: Méiyǒu kǎ kěyǐ lái ma?
刘 勇： 没有 卡 可以 来 吗?

Fúwùyuán: Wánquán kěyǐ, kěyǐ àn cì fù xiànjīn.
服务员： 完全 可以，可以 按 次 付 现金。

Xiǎojié: Jīntiān wǒmen liǎ dōu yòng zhè zhāng kǎ, xíng bù xíng?
小杰： 今天 我们 俩 都 用 这 张 卡，行 不 行?

Fúwùyuán: Kěyǐ, liǎng gè rén jiù shì liǎng cì.
服务员：可以，两 个 人 就 是 两 次。

Liú Yǒng: Jiànshēnzhōngxīn lǐ dōu yǒu shénme ne?

刘 勇： 健身中心 里都有 什么 呢?

Fúwùyuán: Nà kě duō le, yǒu yóuyǒngchí, bǎolíngqiúguǎn,

服务员：那可多了，有 游泳池、 保龄球馆、

pīngpāngqiúshì, jiànshēnfáng shénmede.

乒乓球室、 健身房 什么 的。

Liú Yǒng: Yǒu sāngnáshì ma?

刘 勇： 有 桑拿室 吗?

Fúwùyuán: Yǒu, hái yǒu ànmóshì, zúliáoshì shénmede.

服务员： 有，还 有 按摩室、足疗室 什么 的。

Xiǎojié: Tài hǎo le! Wǒmen jìnqù ba.

小杰： 太好 了! 我们 进去 吧。

Fúwùyuán: Nàbiān hái yǒu yī gè xiūxishì, kěyǐ hē chá, hē kāfēi.

服务员： 那边 还有 一个 休息室,可以 喝 茶、喝 咖啡。

Liú Yǒng: Hǎo de, xièxie nǐ a.

刘 勇： 好 的，谢谢 你 啊。

Liú Yǒng: Nǐ xiǎng xiān qù nǎr?

刘 勇： 你 想 先 去 哪儿?

Xiǎojié: Zánmen xiān qù dǎ bǎolíngqiú, zěnmeyàng?

小杰： 咱们 先 去 打 保龄球，怎么样?

Liú Yǒng: Chéng a, bùguò bǎolíngqiú wǒ kě bù xíng.
刘 勇： 成 啊，不过 保龄球 我 可 不 行。

Xiǎojié: Yàobù, qù dǎ pīngpāngqiú?
小杰： 要不，去 打 乒乓球？

Liú Yǒng: Zhǔyào kàn nǐ, wǒ shénme dōu xíng.
刘 勇： 主要 看 你，我 什么 都 行。

Xiǎojié: Pīngpāngqiú wǒ yě tǐng náshǒu de, xiǎo shíhou chángcháng
小杰： 乒乓球 我 也 挺 拿手 的，小时候 常常

hé bàba yìqǐ dǎ.
和 爸爸 一起 打。

Liú Yǒng: Nà hǎo, zánmen liǎ bǐshi bǐshi, wǒ kě shì Zhōngguórén a!
刘 勇： 那 好，咱们 俩 比试 比试，我 可是 中国人 啊！

Xiǎojié: Xiān bié chuīniú, zánmen shìshi kàn!
小杰： 先 别 吹牛，咱们 试试 看！

Xiǎojié: Wǒ yíng la!
小杰： 我 赢 啦！

Liú Yǒng: Lèi sǐ le, lái, xiūxi yīhuìr.
刘 勇： 累 死 了，来，休息 一会儿。

Liú Yǒng: Lái, hē diǎnr shuǐ.
刘 勇： 来，喝 点儿 水。

Xiǎojié: Jīntiān zhēn guòyǐn.
小杰: 今天 真 过瘾。

Xiǎojié: Nǐ huì gōngfu ma?
小杰: 你会 功夫 吗?

Liú Yǒng: "Gōngfu"? Nǐ shuō de shì "wǔgōng" ba. Nà wǒ kě
刘勇: "功夫"? 你 说 的 是 "武功" 吧。那我可

bù huì.
不会。

Xiǎojié: Ài, wǒ hái yǐwéi Zhōngguórén dōu huì gōngfu ne!
小杰: 唉,我还以为 中国人 都 会 功夫 呢!

Staff: Hello, welcome!

Xiaojie: Can we use this card?

Staff: Yes, it's a per-visit card.

Liu Yong: How many times can this card be used?

Staff: This card is for 30 visits.

Liu Yong: Can you come without a card?

Staff: Certainly, you can pay per visit with cash.

Xiaojie: Can the two of us use this card today?

Staff: Yes, two people would count as two visits.

Liu Yong: What facilities does the fitness center have?

Staff: Plenty, we have a swimming pool, bowling alley, table tennis hall, gym.

Liu Yong: Is there a sauna room?

Staff: Sure, we also have massage rooms, foot reflexogy room and more.

Xiaojie: That's great! Let's go in.

Staff: There's a rest area over there, you can have a tea or coffee.

Liu Yong: Great, thank you.

Liu Yong: Where do you want to go first?

Xiaojie: How about we go bowling first?

Liu Yong: Sure, but I'm no good at bowling.

Xiaojie: Or what about playing table tennis?

Liu Yong: It's up to you, I'm up for anything.

Xiaojie: I'm pretty good at table tennis, I used to play with my dad a lot when I was little.

Liu Yong: OK, let's have a go, I'm Chinese you know!

Xiaojie: Stop bragging, let's play!

Xiaojie: I won!

Liu Yong: I'm exhausted, come on, have a break.

Liu Yong: Here, have some water.

Xiaojie: That was awesome.

Xiaojie: Do you know "Kung Fu"?

Liu Yong: "Kung Fu"? You're talking about Martial Arts. That I don't know.

Xiaojie: I thought all Chinese people knew Kung Fu!

旅游汉语

生词（New Words）

1. 使用	shǐyòng	动	use
2. 完全	wánquán	副	completely
3. 按	àn	介	according to
4. 现金	xiànjīn	名	cash
5. 健身	jiànshēn	动	keep fit
6. 游泳池	yóuyǒngchí	名	swimming pool
7. 保龄球	bǎolíngqiú	名	bowling
8. 乒乓球	pīngpāngqiú	名	table tennis
9. 什么的	shénmede		and so on
10. 桑拿	sāngná	名	sauna
11. 足疗	zúliáo	名	foot massage
12. 休息室	xiūxishì	名	lounge
13. 喝	hē	动	drink
14. 茶	chá	名	tea
15. 主要	zhǔyào	形	main

16. 拿手	náshǒu	形	good at
17. 常常	chángcháng	副	often
18. 比试	bǐshi	动	have a contest
19. 吹牛	chuīniú	动	brag
20. 赢	yíng	动	win
21. 死	sǐ	形	die
22. 过瘾	guòyǐn	动	enjoy oneself to the full
23. 功夫	gōngfu	名	Kung Fu
24. 武功	wǔgōng	名	martial arts skills
25. 以为	yǐwéi	动	mistakenly believe something

注释（Notes）

1. 完全可以。

Absolutely. No problem at all.

2. 那可多了。

Remember we learned in a previous lesson about using 可 to emphasize a point.

3. 还有按摩室、足疗室什么的。

We have a massage room, foot massage and so on. 什么的 is used to indicate and so on, and what not.

4. 要不，去打乒乓球？

Then why don't we play table tennis instead? 要不 is like saying "well then, how about something else".

5. 先别吹牛，咱们试试看！

Don't just boast, let's try and see.

6. 咱们俩比试比试。

Let's have a contest.

7. 我还以为中国人都会功夫呢！

I thought all Chinese could do Kung Fu!

Doing Sports in China

Chinese are very fond of sports and exercise, and not just because the Olympics are coming to China. In many parks in China you can see people engaged in their daily exercises, like "太极拳" *Taiji*, and other traditional forms of exercise. The best time to see this is in the early morning. Most people will be very welcoming if you want to join in and learn some moves yourself. Many parks also have exercise equipment and even pingpong tables or basketball hoops that are available for anyone to use. This is a great way to meet local residents and get some exercise.

Apart from exercising in hotels, you can also go to one of the many fitness clubs that are popular now, especially in the larger cities. Some of these are open for individual visits, or pay-as-you-go. Others may require some type of membership fee and annual dues.

If you check out some of the tourist magazines in cities like Beijing and Shanghai, you can also find running, bicycling and other sports clubs that are always looking for new members.

旅游汉语

 ## 语言点（Bookmarks）

1. 完全 completely

我完全同意你的看法。

I absolutely agree with your viewpoint.

这句话我完全不懂。

I don't understand that sentence at all.

2. 什么的 and so on

他对中国文化感兴趣，喜欢中国书法、中国画什么的。

He is interested in Chinese culture. He likes Chinese calligraphy, Chinese painting and so on.

我们去过中国很多的城市，像北京、上海、广州什么的。

We've been to many cities in China before, like Beijing, Shanghai, Guangzhou and so on.

3. 以为 mistakenly believe something

他汉语说得很好，我们都以为他是中国人呢。

His Chinese is really good. We all thought he was Chinese.

我以为今天会下雨，所以带了雨伞。

I thought it was going to rain today, so I brought an umbrella.

句型与替换练习
(Substitution & Extention)

1. 要不 in that case

要不咱们去吃上海菜吧，四川菜太辣了。

Why don't we go and have Shanghai food? Sichuan food is too hot.

替换例句：

要不我们别去哈尔滨了，那儿太冷了。

要不我们打车去吧，公共汽车太慢了。

去游泳
Go Swimming

旅游汉语

课文 (Text)

表姐： Biǎojiě: Xiǎojié a, guòlái xiē huìr ba! Lèi le ba, zuótiān hé
小杰 啊，过来 歇 会儿 吧! 累 了 吧，昨天 和

biǎogē wánr de zěnmeyàng?
表哥 玩儿 得 怎么样?

小杰： Xiǎojié: Biǎogē dài wǒ qù jiànshēnzhōngxīn dǎ le pīngpāngqiú,
表哥 带 我 去 健身中心 打 了 乒乓球，

nǐ cāi shuí yíng le?
你 猜 谁 赢 了?

表姐： Biǎojiě: Ràng wǒ cāicai, shì biǎogē ba?
让 我 猜猜，是 表哥 吧?

小杰： Xiǎojié: Hāha, bù shì, shì wǒ yíng la, zhēn guòyǐn.
哈哈，不 是，是 我 赢 啦，真 过瘾。

表姐： Biǎojiě: Kàn nǐ, zhème déyì.
看 你，这么 得意。

小杰： Xiǎojié: Dāngrán la.
当然 啦。

表姐： Biǎojiě: Nà nǐ jīntiān hái xiǎng qù dǎ pīngpāngqiú ma?
那 你 今天 还 想 去 打 乒乓球 吗?

小杰： Xiǎojié: Bù xiǎng qù le. Duì le, nǐ xǐhuan yóuyǒng ma?
不 想 去 了。对 了，你 喜欢 游泳 吗?

表姐：Biǎojiě: Xǐhuan a, yóuyǒng kěyǐ jiǎnféi, jùshuō, jīngcháng
喜欢 啊，游泳 可以 减肥，据说，经常

yóuyǒng hái kěyǐ ràng rén biàn de gèng cōngming ne.
游泳 还可以让人变得更 聪明 呢。

小杰：Xiǎojié: Zhēn de ma? Jiànshēnzhōngxīn nàr jiù yǒu yóuyǒngchí.
真 的 吗？ 健身中心 那儿 就 有 游泳池。

表姐：Biǎojiě: Wǒ zhīdao, wǒ zuótiān gāng qùguò, wǒ jīntiān hái yào
我 知道，我 昨天 刚 去过，我 今天 还 要

zài qù yóu.
再 去 游。

小杰：Xiǎojié: Nà wǒ gēn nín yīqǐ qù ba, wǒ hěn jiǔ dōu méi yóuyǒng le.
那 我 跟 您 一起 去 吧，我 很 久 都 没 游泳了。

表姐：Biǎojiě: Kěyǐ ya. Nǐ dài yóuyǒngyī le ma?
可以 呀。你 带 游泳衣 了 吗？

小杰：Xiǎojié: Méiyǒu, zhè kě zěnmebàn na?
没有，这 可 怎么办 呐？

表姐：Biǎojiě: Méishìr, jiànshēnzhōngxīn yǒu mài de, wǒmen kěyǐ dào
没事儿，健身中心 有 卖 的，我们 可以 到

nàr mǎi yī jiàn.
那儿 买 一 件。

小杰：Xiǎojié: Tài hǎo le, wǒmen zǒu ba.
太 好 了，我们 走 吧。

表姐：Biǎojiě: Xiǎojié, nǐ kàn, zhèr bù shì yǒu hěn duō yóuyǒngyī ma?
小杰，你 看，这儿 不 是 有 很 多 游泳衣 吗？

小杰： Ràng wǒ kànkan, dōu tǐng piàoliang de.
小杰： 让 我 看看，都 挺 漂亮 的。

服务员： Nín hǎo!
服务员： 您 好!

表姐： Nín hǎo, wǒmen xiǎng mǎi yī jiàn yóuyǒngyī, yī gè yǒngmào.
表姐： 您 好，我们 想 买 一件 游泳衣、一 个 泳帽。

小杰： Hái yǒu yī fù yǒng jìng.
小杰： 还 有 一 副 泳 镜。

服务员： Yóuyǒngyī nín yào nǎ yī jiàn?
服务员： 游泳衣 您 要 哪 一件?

表姐： Xiǎojié, xǐhuan nǎ yī jiàn?
表姐： 小杰，喜欢 哪 一件?

小杰： Wǒ xǐhuan nà jiàn lánsè de.
小杰： 我 喜欢 那件 蓝色 的。

服务员： Lái, gěi nín dōngxi.
服务员： 来，给 您 东西。

表姐： Xièxie. Lái, Xiǎojié, zánmen zǒu.
表姐： 谢谢。来，小杰，咱们 走。

小杰： Nà lǐbian de yóuyǒngchí dà ma?
小杰： 那里边 的 游泳池 大 吗?

表姐： Shì biāozhǔnchí, yǒu 50 mǐ cháng.
表姐： 是 标准池，有 50 米 长。

小杰： Yǒu qiǎnshuǐchí ma?
小杰： 有 浅水池 吗?

表姐: Zǒu ba,　jìnqù kànkan jiù zhīdao le.
表姐： 走 吧，进去 看看 就 知道 了。

表姐: Xiǎojié, zhèbian shì qiǎnshuǐqū, nàbian shì shēnshuǐqū.
表姐： 小杰，这边 是 浅水区，那边 是 深水区。

小杰: Wǒ háishi xiān zài qiǎnshuǐ zhèbian yóu ba.
小杰： 我 还是 先 在 浅水 这边 游 吧。

表姐: Xiǎojié, dào wǒ zhèbian lái yóu ba.
表姐： 小杰，到 我 这边 来 游 吧。

小杰: Nǐ nàbian de shēnshuǐ yǒu duō shēn?
小杰： 你 那边 的 深水 有 多 深？

表姐: Liǎng mǐ zuǒyòu ba,　guòlái shìshi?
表姐： 两 米 左右 吧，过来 试试？

小杰: Wǒ yóuyǒng de jìshù bù tài hǎo, bù gǎn dào tài shēn
小杰： 我 游泳 的 技术 不太 好，不 敢 到 太 深

de dìfāng qù yóuyǒng.
的 地方 去 游泳。

表姐: Yào bù,　zài gěi nǐ mǎi gè yóuyǒngquān?
表姐： 要 不，再 给 你 买 个 游泳圈？

小杰: Wǒ háishi xiān shìshi ba
小杰： 我 还是 先 试试 吧。

表姐: Xiǎojié, xiǎoxīn! Zhè bù shì yóu de tǐng hǎo de ma.
表姐： 小杰，小心! 这 不 是 游得 挺 好 的 嘛。

Xiao Jie, come and swim at my end.

Consin: Xiaojie, are you tired? Have a rest! Xiaojie, how did it go with your cousin yesterday?

Xiaojie: My cousin took me to play table tennis at the sports centre. Guess who won?

Consin: Let me guess. Did your cousin win?

Xiaojie: Haha. No, I won and I felt awesome.

Consin: Look at you, so pleased with yourself!

Xiaojie: Of course.

Consin: Well, do you still want to play table tennis today?

Xiaojie: Not really. Do you like swimming?

Consin: Sure. Swimming is good for losing weight. Some people even say swimming a lot can make you smarter.

Xiaojie: Really? There's a swimming pool at the sports centre.

Consin: I know. I was there yesterday. I'm going swimming again today.

Xiaojie: How about I come with you? I haven't swum for ages.

Consin: Sure. You can. Xiaojie, have you brought your bathing suit?

Xiaojie: No. What are we going to do?

Consin: Not a problem. They sell bathing suits at the sports centre. We can buy one there.

Xiaojie: That's great. Let's go.

Consin: Xiaojie, look at all those bathing suits!

Xiaojie: Let me have a look. They're all so pretty!

Salesperson: Hello!

Consin: Hi, I'd like to buy a bathing suit and a swimming cap.

Xiaojie: Plus a pair of goggles.

Salesperson: Which bathing suit would you like?

Consin: Xiaojie, which one do you like?

Xiaojie: I like the blue one.

Salesperson: Here you are. Take care.

Consin: Thanks. Come on. Xiaojie, let's go.

Xiaojie: Is the swimming pool big?

Consin: It's standard size, 50 metres long.

Xiaojie: Is there a shallow pool there?

Consin: We'll know once we get in.

Consin: Xiaojie, the pool's shallow at this end and deep at the other end.

Xiaojie: I think I'll swim at the shallow end first.

Consin: Xiaojie, come and swim at my end.

Xiaojie: How deep is the water over there?

Consin: Around two metres. Will you come and try it?

Xiaojie: I'm not good at swimming. I'm a bit scared about swimming in deep water.

Consin: How about I buy you a safety ring?

Xiaojie: I'll have a try first.

Consin: Xiaojie, be careful! You're doing just fine.

旅游汉语

生词（New Words）

1. 歇	xiē	动	have a rest
2. （一）会儿	(yī)huìr	名	a while
3. 昨天	zuótiān	名	yesterday
4. 表哥	biǎogē	名	elder male cousin
5. 猜	cāi	动	guess
6. 得意	déyì	形	pleased with oneself
7. 减肥	jiǎnféi	动	lose weight
8. 据说	jùshuō	连	it is said
9. 经常	jīngcháng	副	often
10. 聪明	cōngming	形	clever
11. 漂亮	piàoliang	形	pretty
12. 泳镜	yǒngjìng	名	swimming goggles
13. 标准	biāozhǔn	形	standard
14. 浅	qiǎn	形	shallow
15. 深	shēn	形	deep

16. 区	qū	名	area
17. 技术	jìshù	名	skill
18. 敢	gǎn	动	dare
19. 小心	xiǎoxīn	动	be careful

旅游汉语

注释（Notes）

1. 看你，这么得意。

Look at you, so pleased with yourself. 得意 is often used in a negative sense, to be complacent, conceited. But it can be used in a positive way as well. 最得意的学生 favourite student, 最得意的作品 favourite work, some kind of composition that you are most proud of.

2. 据说游泳还可以让人变得更聪明呢。

据说，it is said, or I hear. 据 is short for 根据 and literally means "according to". I hear that swimming can even make people smarter. 变得 is to become. 变得更聪明，become more intelligent. The 呢 at the end of the sentence serves to reinforce this assertion. It doesn't play a critical role in changing the meaning of the sentence, and is used mainly for tone of voice.

3. 我昨天刚去过。

I was just there yesterday. 过 is used after a verb to indicate that the action happened in the past and was completed. I've been there before, 我去过. Adding 刚 indicates that this was very recent.

4. 我很久都没游泳了。

I haven't gone swimming for a long time. Here, 都 adds a little emphasis. You could say 我很久没有游泳. It means the same thing, I haven't been swimming for a long time, but it lacks the emphasis of 我很久都没有游泳.

5. 这儿不是有很多游泳衣吗?

We're going to look at this pattern today, using 不是 something 吗 to ask a question. This is used when the answer to the question is obvious, or when you think you know the answer already. 不是吗? Isn't it so? 这儿不是有吗? Don't they have them here? You might ask this when you see something right in front of you. In this case, the meaning is more like "what did I tell you, here they are". 这不是游得挺好吗? Isn't she swimming quite well? Again, using the 不是 something 吗 pattern indicates a rhetorical question. The answer is obvious to see.

旅游汉语

 ## 语言点（Bookmarks）

1. 据说 according to

据说去上海的机票很便宜。

I hear that the plane ticket to Shanghai is really cheap.

据说他会说好几门外语。

I hear that he can speak many foreign languages.

句型与替换练习
（Substitution & Extention）

1. V+ 过 the action happened in the past

你看过京剧吗?

Have you ever seen Peking Opera before?

替换例句:

你吃过北京烤鸭吗?

他去过很多国家旅游。

2. 不是……吗 isn't it so

去长城的车不是早上六点开吗?

Isn't it true that the car or train to the Great Wall leaves at six in the morning?

替换例句:

这件衣服不是你的吗?

你不是已经去过上海了吗?

准备离开

Prepare To Leave

旅游汉语

课文（Text）

Qiántái: Nín hǎo!
前台：您 好！

Huáng Rénháo: Nín hǎo! Míngtiān wǒmen yào líkāi, qǐng wèn zuì wǎn
黄 人豪：您 好！ 明天 我们 要 离开，请 问 最 晚

shénme shíhou kěyǐ jiézhàng?
什么 时候 可以 结账？

Qiántái: Míngtiān zhōngwǔ 12diǎn yǐqián, chāoguò 12diǎn xūyào
前台：明天 中午 12点 以前，超过 12点 需要

jiāshōu bàntiān de fángfèi.
加收 半天 的 房费。

Huáng Rénháo: Wǒ míngtiān děi 1diǎn duō cái néng líkāi, nà zěnme
黄 人豪：我 明天 得1点 多 才 能 离开，那 怎么

bàn cái hǎo ne?
办 才 好 呢？

Qiántái: Nín kěyǐ 12diǎn yǐqián tuìfáng, xíngli kěyǐ fàng zài
前台：您 可以 12点 以前 退房，行李 可以 放 在

jìcúnchù.
寄存处。

Huáng Rénháo: Hǎo! Jiù zhème bàn! Wǒ hái yǒu yī gè wèntí, míngtiān

黄　人豪： 好! 就 这么 办! 我 还有 一个 问题, 明天

zǎochén wǒ kěyǐ zǎodiǎnr guòlái ná zhàngdān ma?

早晨 我 可以 早点儿 过来 拿 账单 吗?

Qiántái: Kěyǐ.

前台： 可以。

Huáng Rénháo: Wǒmen yào héduì yīxià.

黄　人豪： 我们 要 核对 一下。

Qiántái: Xiānsheng, nín de fángjiānhào shì?

前台： 先生, 您 的 房间号 是?

Huáng Rénháo: 918 fángjiān hé 1179 fángjiān, liǎng gè fángjiān dōu yào

黄　人豪： 918 房间 和 1179 房间, 两 个 房间 都 要

jiézhàng.

结账。

Qiántái: Míngtiān shàngwǔ, wǒmen huì bǎ zhàngdān gěi nín

前台： 明天 上午, 我们 会 把 账单 给 您

zhǔnbèi hǎo.

准备 好。

Huáng Rénháo: Xièxie! Lìngwài wǒmen míngtiān shàngwǔ xiǎng zài

黄　人豪： 谢谢! 另外 我们 明天 上午 想 在

fángjiān lǐ yòng zǎocān.

房间 里 用 早餐。

Qiántái: Méi wèntí, nín kěyǐ dǎ kèfángbù de diànhuà, zài fángjiān
前台：没问题，您可以打客房部的电话，在房间

de diànhuà shàng zhíjiē bō "8", nín jiù kěyǐ zhíjiē yùdìng
的电话上直接拨"8"，您就可以直接预订

zǎocān le. Lìngwài, nín yě kěyǐ zài wǒmen zhèr dìng.
早餐了。另外，您也可以在我们这儿订。

Huáng Rénháo: Ō, míngtiān wǒ hái xūyào jiàozǎofúwù.
黄　人豪：噢，明天我还需要叫早服务。

Qiántái: Kěyǐ, qǐngwèn jǐ diǎn?
前台：可以，请问几点?

Huáng Rénháo: 7 diǎn.
黄　人豪：7点。

Qiántái: Fángjiān hàomǎ shì 918 ba?
前台：房间号码是918吧?

Huáng Rénháo: Bù, shì 1179 fángjiān, qiānwàn bié wàng le.
黄　人豪：不，是1179房间，千万别忘了。

Qiántái: Míngtiān zǎo 7 diǎn jiào 1179 fángjiān qǐchuáng.
前台：明天早7点叫1179房间起床。

Huáng Rénháo: Duì, xièxie!
黄　人豪：对，谢谢!

Huáng Rénháo: Xuěméi, dōu bàn hǎo le.
黄　人豪：雪梅，都 办 好 了。

Xuěméi: Tài hǎo le! Fángzi zhōngyú zhǎo hǎo le, wǒmen zài Běijīng
雪梅：太 好 了! 房子 终于 找 好 了, 我们 在 北京

yǒu zìjǐ　de jiā le.
有自己的家了。

Huáng Rénháo: Jīntiān děi bǎ dōngxi dōu shōushi hǎo, qiānwàn bié làxià dōngxi.
黄　人豪：今天得把东西都 收拾 好，千万 别落下东西。

Xuěméi: Zhǔyào shì Xiǎojié de dōngxi, nǐ gěi tā dǎ gè diànhuà
雪梅：主要 是 小杰 的 东西，你 给 她 打 个 电话

ba, ràng tā hǎohāo zhěnglǐ zhěnglǐ.
吧，让 她 好好 整理 整理。

Huáng Rénháo: Nǐ qù tā de fángjiān kànkan ba, bāngbang tā.
黄　人豪：你去 她 的 房间 看看 吧，帮帮 她。

Xuěméi: Hǎo de.
雪梅：好 的。

Huáng Rénháo: Bié wàng le gàosu tā, míngtiān zǎoshang lái chī fàn.
黄　人豪：别 忘了告诉她，明天 早上 来吃饭。

Xuěméi: Hǎo de.
雪梅：好的。

Front desk: Hello!

Huang Renhao: Hello! We're leaving tomorrow. When is the latest time I could check out?

Front desk: Before noon tomorrow, you'll be charged half a day's room rate after 12.

Huang Renhao: But I can only leave after 1'o clock tomorrow, what should I do?

Front desk: You can check out before 12, but leave the luggage with the concierge.

Huang Renhao: Great! That's what I'll do! One more question, can I come a bit earlier tomorrow morning to get the bill?

Front desk: Sure.

Huang Renhao: We need to check it.

Front desk: Sir, your room number is...?

Huang Renhao: Rooms 918 and 1179, we need to check out of both rooms.

Front desk: We'll have the bills ready for you tomorrow morning.

Huang Renhao: Thank you! Another thing, we'd like to have breakfast in the room tomorrow mornings.

Front desk: Not a problem, you can ring housekeeping to order breakfast just by dialing "8" on the room phone, or you can book here.

Huang Renhao: Oh, we'll also need a wake up call tomorrow.

Front desk: Yes, what time?

Huang Renhao: 7.

Front desk: The room number is 918?

Huang Renhao: No, it's room 1179, please don't forget.

Front desk: Wake up call for room 1179 at 7 tomorrow morning.

Huang Renhao: Thank you!

Huang Renhao: Xuemei! Everything gets fixed!

Xuemei: Great! We've found our apartment, we finally have our own home in Beijing.

Huang Renhao: We need to pack up everything today, we better not leave anything behind.

Xuemei: Mainly Xiaojie's stuff. Why don't you give her a call, ask her to get organized.

Huang Renhao: You should check on her in her room, give her a hand.

Xuemei: OK.

Huang Renhao: Don't forget to tell her to come over for breakfast tomorrow morning.

Xuemei: OK.

旅游汉语

生词（New Words）

1. 离开	líkāi	动	leave
2. 结账	jiézhàng	动	pay
3. 费	fèi	名	fee
4. 以前	yǐqián	名	before
5. 超过	chāoguò	动	exceed
6. 退房	tuìfáng	动	check out
7. 寄存处	jìcúnchù	名	warehouse
8. 账单	zhàngdān	名	bill
9. 核对	héduì	动	check
10. 会	huì	动	will happen
11. 准备	zhǔnbèi	动	prepare
12. 另外	lìngwài	副	in addition
13. 早餐	zǎocān	名	breakfast
14. 直接	zhíjiē	副	directly
15. 服务	fúwù	名	service

16. 起床	qǐchuáng	动	get up
17. 终于	zhōngyú	副	at last, finally
18. 收拾	shōushi	动	put in order
19. 整理	zhěnglǐ	动	arrange

旅游汉语

注释（Notes）

1. 超过12点需要加收半天的房费。

超过 is to exceed, so 超过12点 means after 12 o'clock. 超过12点要加收半天的房费, you have to pay another half day's charge after 12 o'clock.

2. 我们会把账单给您准备好。

会 indicates that an action will happen in the future. We will prepare the bill for you.

3. 您就可以直接预订早餐了。

You can reserve or order breakfast directly. 直接 is directly.

4. 千万别忘了。

Whatever you do, don't forget. 千万 literally means "10 million", but here it is a way of emphasising "no matter what", "make absolutely sure". 千万别落东西, make absolutely sure you don't forget anything, or leave anything behind.

5. 房子终于找好了。

终于 means "finally". We've finally found a home.

6. 得把东西都收拾好。

Collect everything together, pack everything up.

语言点（Bookmarks）

1. 超过 in excess of

为了保护眼睛，每天看电视不能超过1个小时。

To protect your eyes, you should not watch TV more than an hour a day.

今年来中国旅游的外国游客的人数已经超过了去年。

The number of foreign tourists visiting China this year has already exceeded the number last year.

2. 会 something will happen

我已经给他打电话了，他今天会来的。

I already phoned him. He will come today.

这件事他怎么会知道的?

How could he possibly know about this thing?

3. 直接 directly

你以后有事可以直接跟我们联系。

In future, you can contact us directly.

这次我直接从上海去杭州，就不回北京了。

This time we are going to go directly from Shanghai to Hangzhou. We are not going to go back to Beijing.

4. 终于 something has finally happened

我们终于爬上了长城。

We finally have climbed the Great Wall.

我们终于到了北京。

We've finally come to Beijing.

旅游汉语

句型与替换练习
（Substitution & Extention）

1. 千万 no matter what

你骑车上街千万要小心。

When you ride your bike, be sure to be careful.

2. 千万别 mustn't

你千万别忘了带护照。

Whatever you do, don't forget to bring your passport.

替换例句：

那家饭店太贵了，你千万别去。

多穿点衣服吧，千万别感冒。

第16课

退房
Check Out

 课文（Text）

Huáng Rénháo: Xiǎojié ne?
黄 人豪： 小杰 呢？

Xuěméi: Ài, tā qù pāi zhàopiàn le, mǎshàng guòlái.
雪梅： 唉，她去拍 照片了，马上 过来。

Huáng Rénháo: Nín hǎo, wǒmen tuìfáng.
黄 人豪： 您 好，我们 退房。

Qiántái: Qǐng wèn nín tuì nǎ gè fángjiān?
前台： 请 问 您 退 哪个 房间？

Huáng Rénháo: 918 fángjiān hé 1179 fángjiān.
黄 人豪： 918 房间 和 1179 房间。

Qiántái: Qǐng shāo děng yīxiàr, wǒmen xiān qù fángjiān kàn
前台： 请 稍 等 一下儿，我们 先 去 房间 看

yīxiàr, kěyǐ ma?
一下儿，可以 吗？

Qiántái: Xiānsheng, zhè shì 918 fángjiān hé 1179 fángjiān de
前台： 先生， 这 是 918 房间 和 1179 房间 的

zhàngdān, qǐng nín héduì yīxiàr.
账单， 请 您 核对 一下儿。

Huáng Rénháo: Suàn le ba, bù yòng héduì le.
黄 人豪：算 了吧，不 用 核对 了。

Qiántái: Nín háishi héduì yīxiàr ba.
前台：您 还是 核对 一下儿 吧。

Xuěméi: Hǎo de, nà wǒ kànkan. Láojià, yǒu jǐ xiàng wǒ bù tài
雪梅：好 的，那 我 看看。劳驾，有 几项 我 不 太

míngbai.
明白。

Qiántái: Qǐng wèn shì nǎ jǐ xiàng?
前台： 请 问 是 哪 几项？

Xuěméi: Dì-yī xiàng zhèxiàng, xǐyīfèi.
雪梅：第一项 这项，洗衣费。

Qiántái: "Xǐyīfèi, 26 rì", nà tiān nín méiyǒu xǐyīfu, shì ma?
前台："洗衣费, 26日"，那 天 您 没有 洗衣服，是 吗？

Xuěméi: Xǐ le, dànshì kèfángbù de jīnglǐ shuō, nà cì de
雪梅：洗 了，但是 客房部 的 经理 说，那次 的

xǐyī fèiyòng miǎn le.
洗衣 费用 免 了。

Qiántái: Ō, shì zhèyàng. Nín bié zháojí, wǒ gěi nín chácha.
前台：噢，是 这样。您 别 着急，我 给 您 查查。

前台：对不起，您说的对，客房部免收了您
Qiántái: Duìbuqǐ, nín shuō de duì, kèfángbù miǎn shōu le nín

的洗衣费用，非常抱歉！
de xǐyī fèiyòng, fēicháng bàoqiàn!

雪梅：那这项是什么费用呢？
Xuěméi: Nà zhè xiàng shì shénme fèiyòng ne?

前台：让我看看，这是1179房间打碎了一个
Qiántái: Ràng wǒ kànkan, zhè shì 1179 fángjiān dǎ suì le yī gè

茶水杯。
cháshuǐbēi.

黄人豪：我看算了吧，没有其他问题就这样吧。
Huáng Rénháo: Wǒ kàn suàn le ba, méiyǒu qítā wèntí jiù zhèyàng ba.

前台：夫人，对不起！我再给您打一份新的
Qiántái: Fūrén, duìbuqǐ! Wǒ zài gěi nín dǎ yī fèn xīn de

账单，您再核对一下儿。
zhàngdān, nín zài héduì yīxiàr.

前台：没问题的话，请您签个字。
Qiántái: Méi wèntí de huà, qǐng nín qiān gè zì.

雪梅：好的。
Xuěméi: Hǎo de.

Qiántái: Nín yòng shénme fāngshì zhīfù? Xiànjīn háishi xìnyòngkǎ?

前台：您 用 什么 方式 支付? 现金 还是 信用卡?

Xuěméi: Yòng xìnyòngkǎ ba.

雪梅：用 信用卡 吧。

Qiántái: Zhè shì nín de fāpiào, qǐng nín màn zǒu.

前台：这是您的发票，请您慢走。

Huáng Rénháo: Xièxie.

黄 人豪：谢谢。

旅游汉语

Huang Renhao: Where's Xiaojie?

Xuemei: She's gone to take photos, she'll be back in a minute.

Huang Renhao: Hello, we'd like to check out.

Front desk: May I ask which rooms you were in?

Huang Renhao: Rooms 918 and 1179.

Front desk: Please wait a moment. We have to have a look at the rooms first. Is that alright?

Front desk: Sir, these are the bills for rooms 918 and 1179, please check it.

Huang Renhao: Forget it, there's no need.

Front desk: You better check it.

Xuemei: OK, I'll have a look. Excuse me, I'm not sure about a few items.

Front desk: Which items?

Xuemei: The first is this one, laundry charges.

Front desk: "Laundry charges, 26th", so you didn't have any laundry done for that day?

Xuemei: We did, but the housekeeping manager said the charges were waived.

Front desk: Don't worry. I'll check it for you.

Front desk: Sorry, you're right, housekeeping waived your laundry charges. So sorry!

Xuemei: Well, what charge is this?

Front desk: Let me see, there was a broken cup in room 1179 room.

Huang Renhao: Forget about it, if there are no other problems just leave it.

Front desk: Sorry madam! I'll print a new bill for you. Please check it.

Front desk: If there's no problem, please sign it.

Xuemei: OK.

Front desk: How are you paying? Cash or credit card?

Xuemei: Credit card.

Front desk: This is your receipt. Take you time.

Huang Renhao: Thanks.

旅游汉语

生词（New Words）

1. 算了吧	suàn le ba		forget about it
2. 项	xiàng	量	measure word for items
3. 但是	dànshì	连	but, however
4. 查	chá	动	check
5. 碎	suì	形	broken
6. 茶	chá	名	tea
7. 杯	bēi	名	cup
8. 其他	qítā	代	others
9. 新	xīn	形	new
10. 方式	fāngshì	名	way, pattern
11. 支付	zhīfù	动	pay
12. 信用卡	xìnyòngkǎ	名	credit card

注释 (Notes)

1. 请您核对一下儿吧。

Please take a moment to double-check. We learned this phrase in the previous lesson. By adding 一下儿 after a verb, it softens the tone. 打听一下儿, to inquire about.

2. 您还是核对一下儿吧。

还是 in this instance is used to emphasize a suggestion, like I really think you should check the bill.

3. 劳驾，有几项我不太明白。

劳驾 is a polite way of getting someone's attention, like "excuse me" or "may I trouble you". 有几项我不太明白, there are a few items I don't fully understand. 项 is the measure word for items. To get someone's attention, instead of 劳驾 we could say 请问 may I ask, or 打扰一下 can I trouble you a moment.

4. 那次的洗衣费用免了。

There would be no charge for the laundry that time. Remember that there was a problem with the laundry? Instead of 费用, which is a more formal expression, we could say 费，as in 洗衣费 laundry charge，停车费 a fee for parking.

5. 非常抱歉。

I'm extremely sorry.

6. 我看算了吧。

I say forget about it, says 黄人豪. In other words, let's just pay for that, it's not important. Here, 我看 doesn't literally mean "I see", it's more like "I think", "in my opinion".

7. 您用什么方式支付?现金还是信用卡?

What will you pay with, cash or credit card? This time, 还是 indicates a choice, cash or credit card.

语言点（Bookmarks）

1. 其他 another person or a thing or an animal

你还有其他的问题吗？

Do you have any other questions?

这些衣服还有其他的颜色吗？

Does this clothing come in any other colors?

2. 劳驾 excuse me

劳驾，请问现在几点了？

Excuse me, could you please tell me what time it is?

劳驾，请问去故宫怎么走？

Excuse me, could you please tell me how to get to the Forbidden City?

旅游汉语

句型与替换练习
(Substitution & Extention)

1. 还是…… use as a suggestion

我们还是坐飞机去那儿，这样比较快。

Let's go there by plane, it's faster that way.

替换例句：

> 我们还是买这件红色的吧，这件衣服好看一些。
>
> 我们还是自己做饭吃吧，这样比较便宜。

2. 算了吧 forget about it

这家饭店太贵了，我看算了吧，我们还是换一家饭店吧。

This restaurant is too expensive. Forget about it. Let's go to a different restaurant.

替换例句：

> 那儿太远了，算了吧，我看今天就别去了。
>
> 这件衣服太贵了，算了吧，我们就别买了。